A Book of Santa's

A hand drawn adult coloring book

A Turners Art and Crafts Production

By

Michael D Turner

Copyright © 2018 Michael D Turner

All rights reserved.

No part of this book may be reproduced, transmitted, or stored in any form or by any means except for your own personal use or for a book review, without the express, written permission of the author:

turnersartandcrafts@gmail.com

Other books by Michael D Turner

Cats in Big Hats

eMpTy Idea Book: A book to get things done.

Digital downloads available at: https://www.etsy.com/shop/TurnersArtAndCrafts

Along with my other projects.

I hope you enjoy coloring my drawing as much as I enjoyed drawing them.

Thank you for your purchases.

Colorist's
Name _____

Date Started _____

Date Completed _____

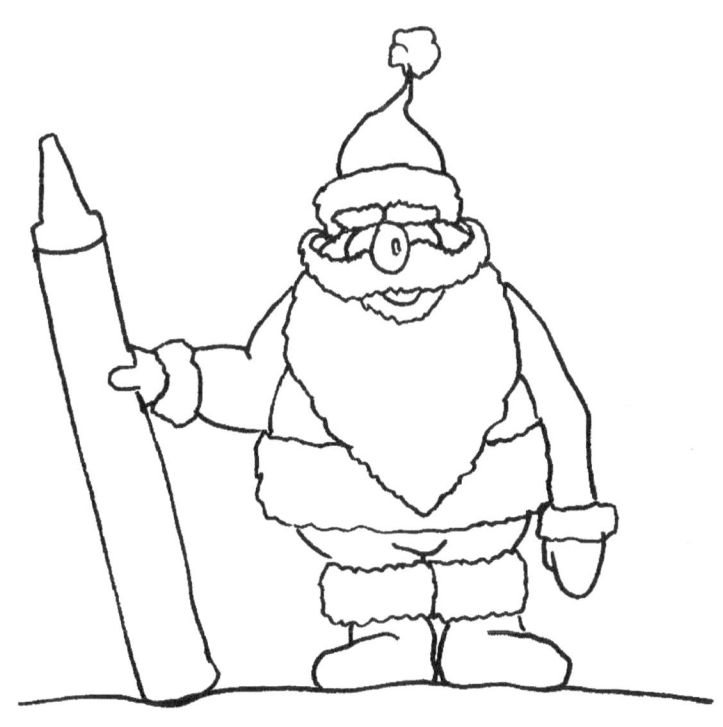

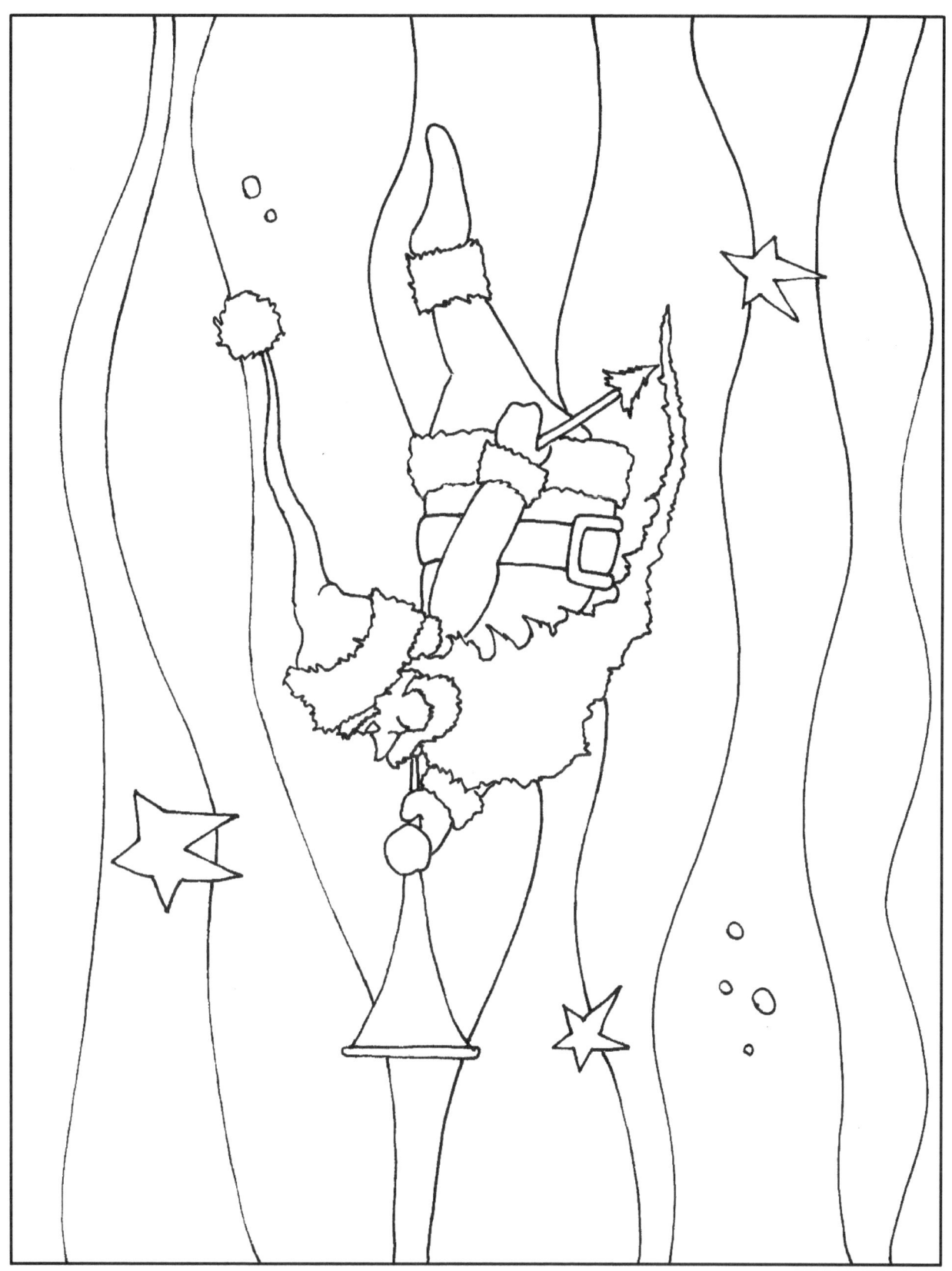

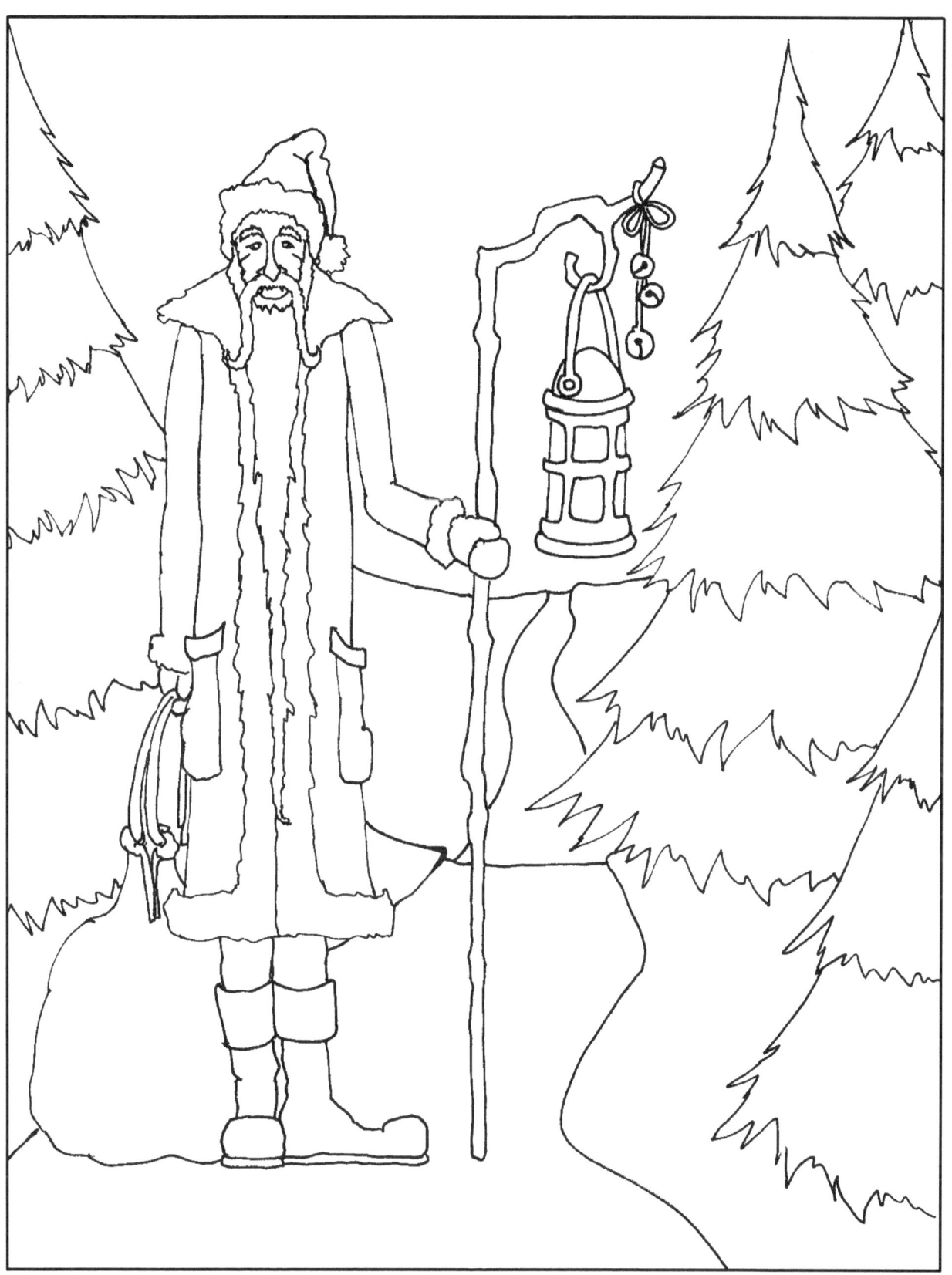

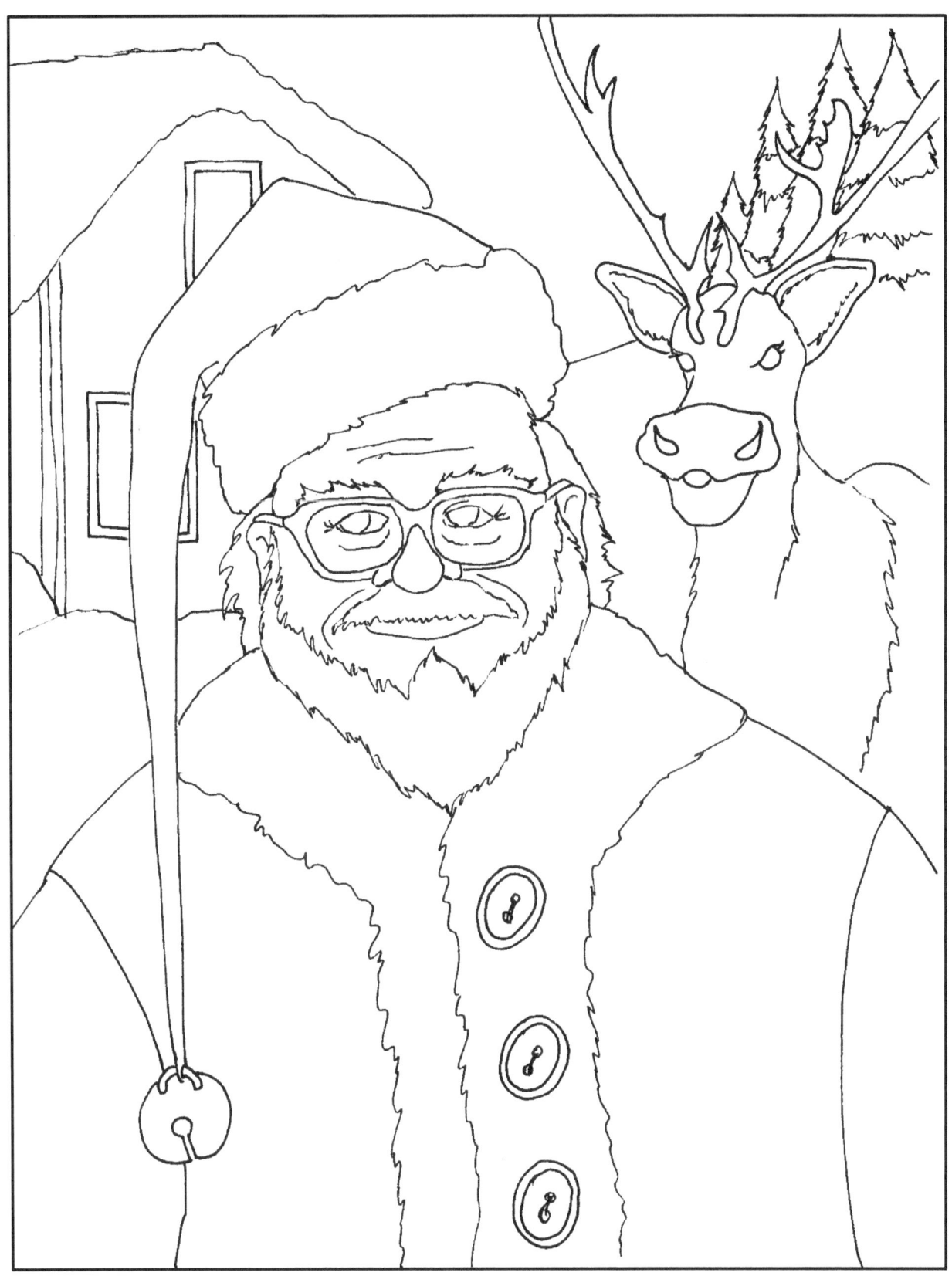

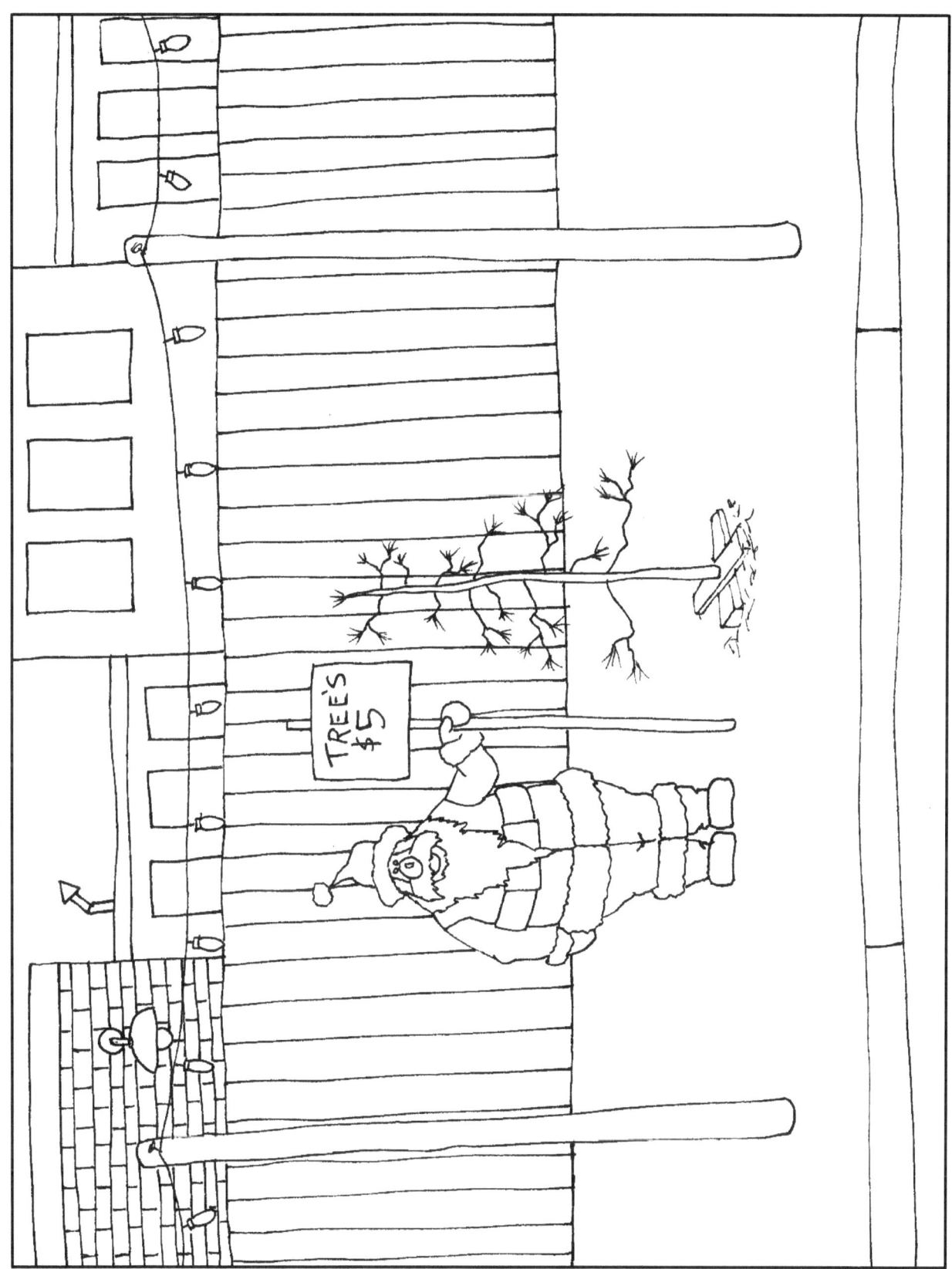

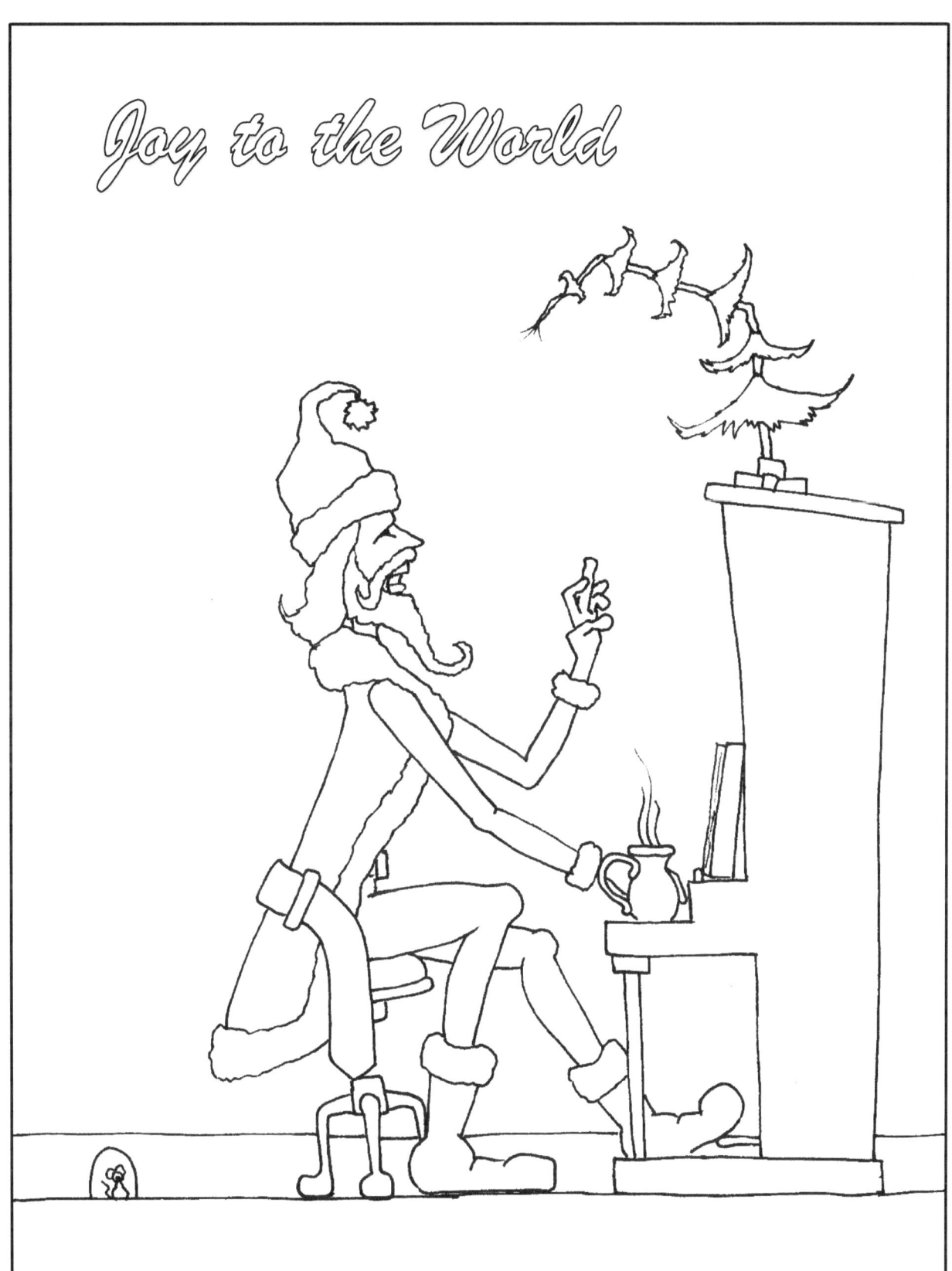

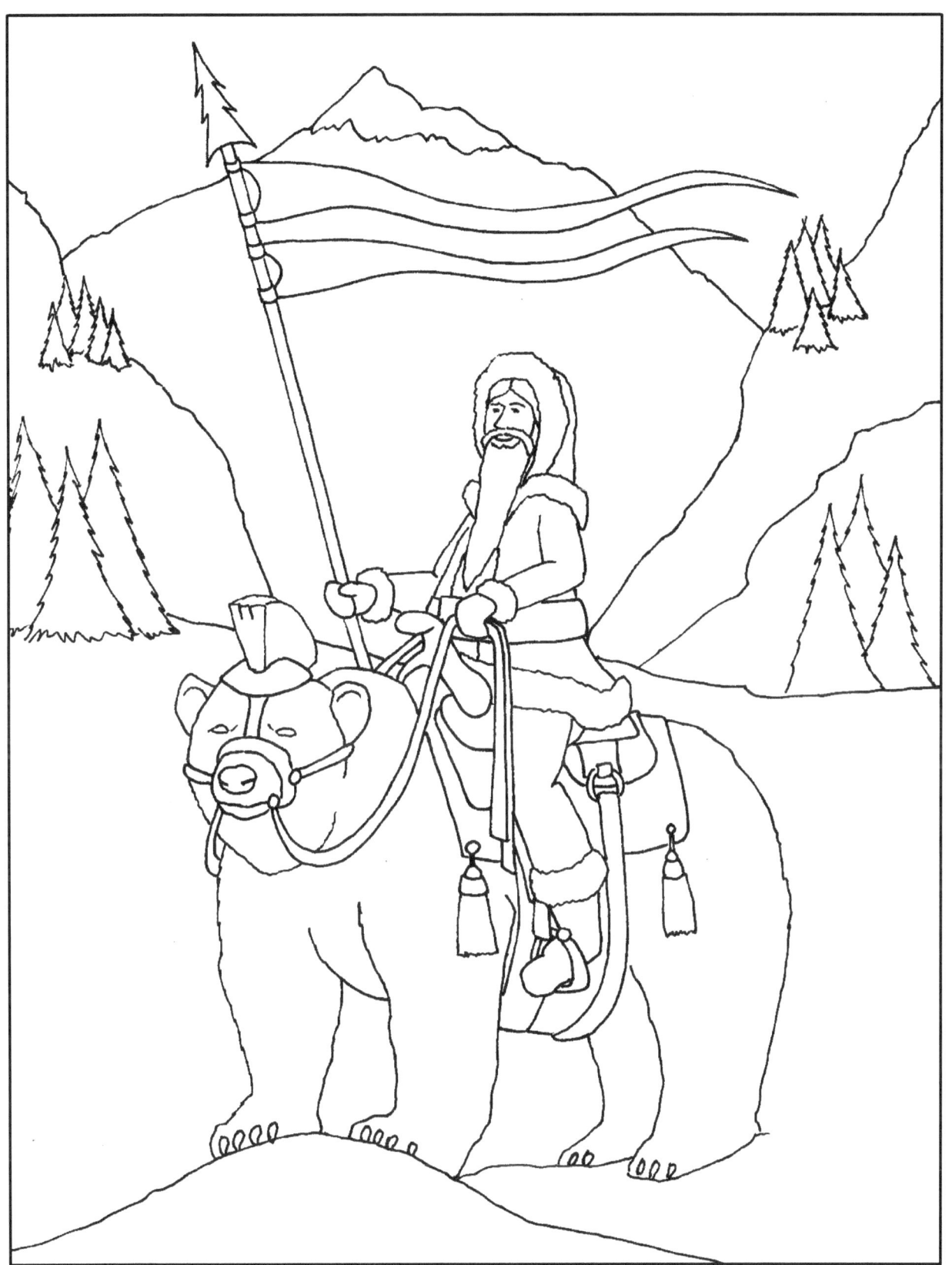

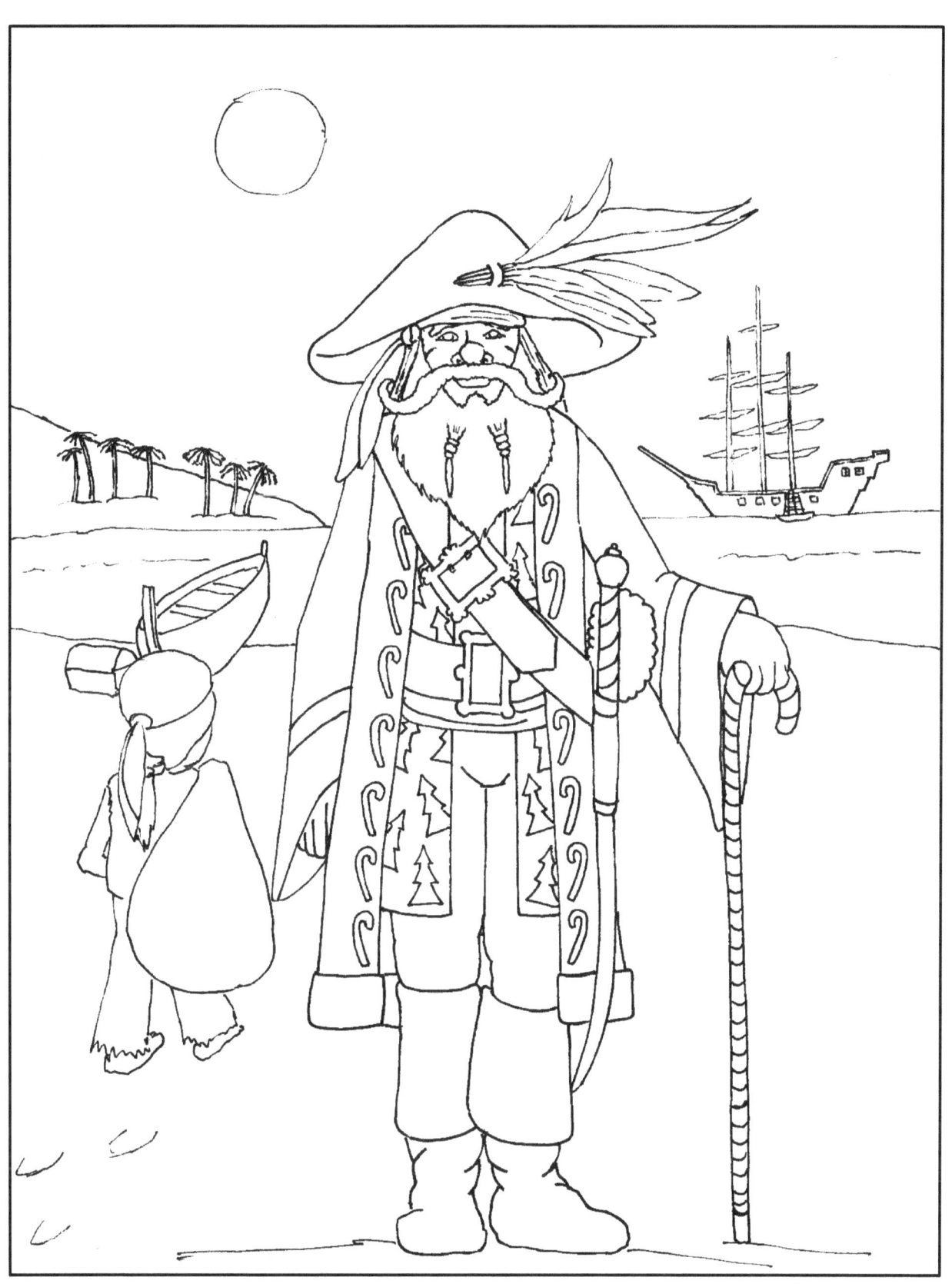

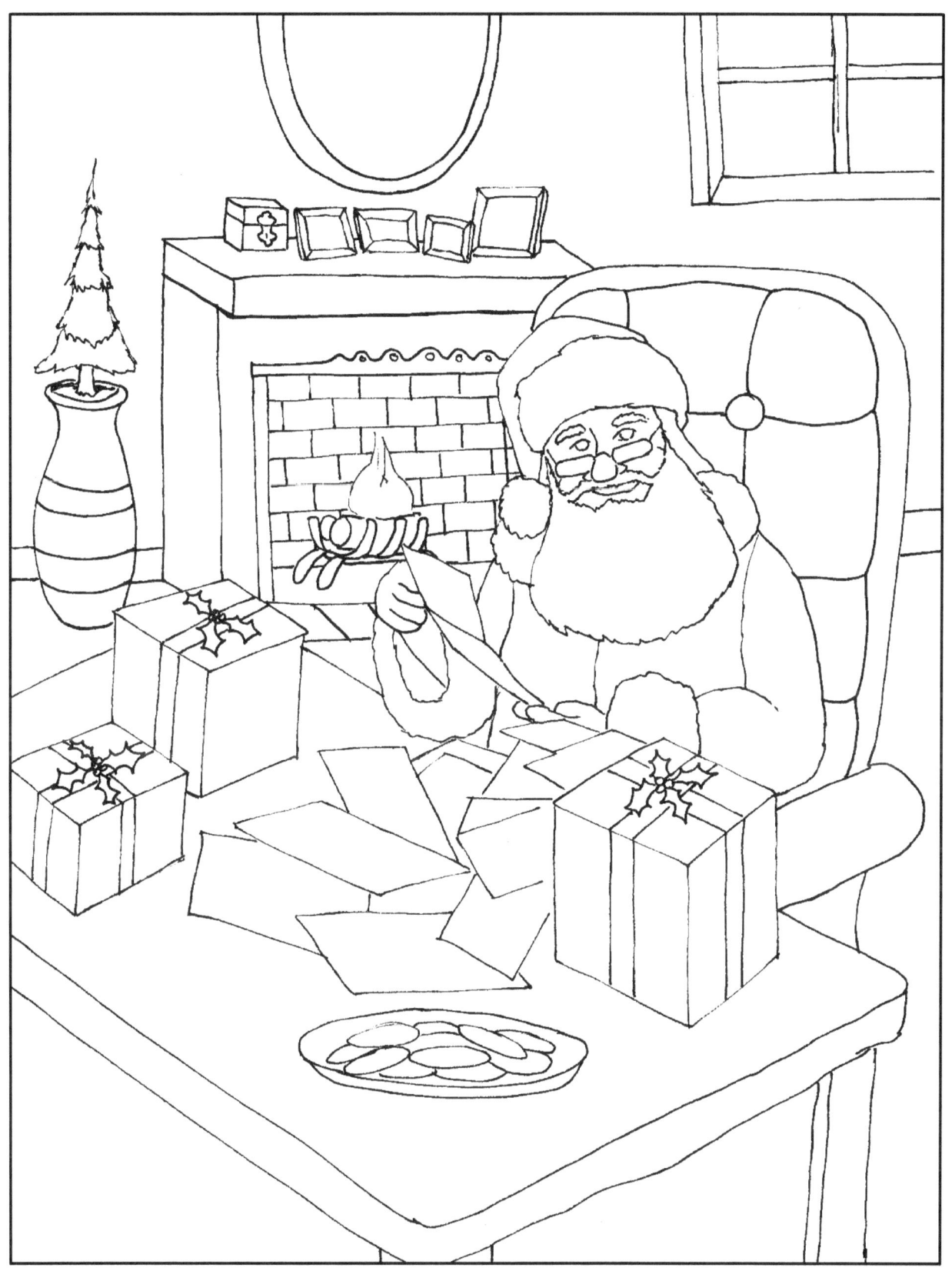

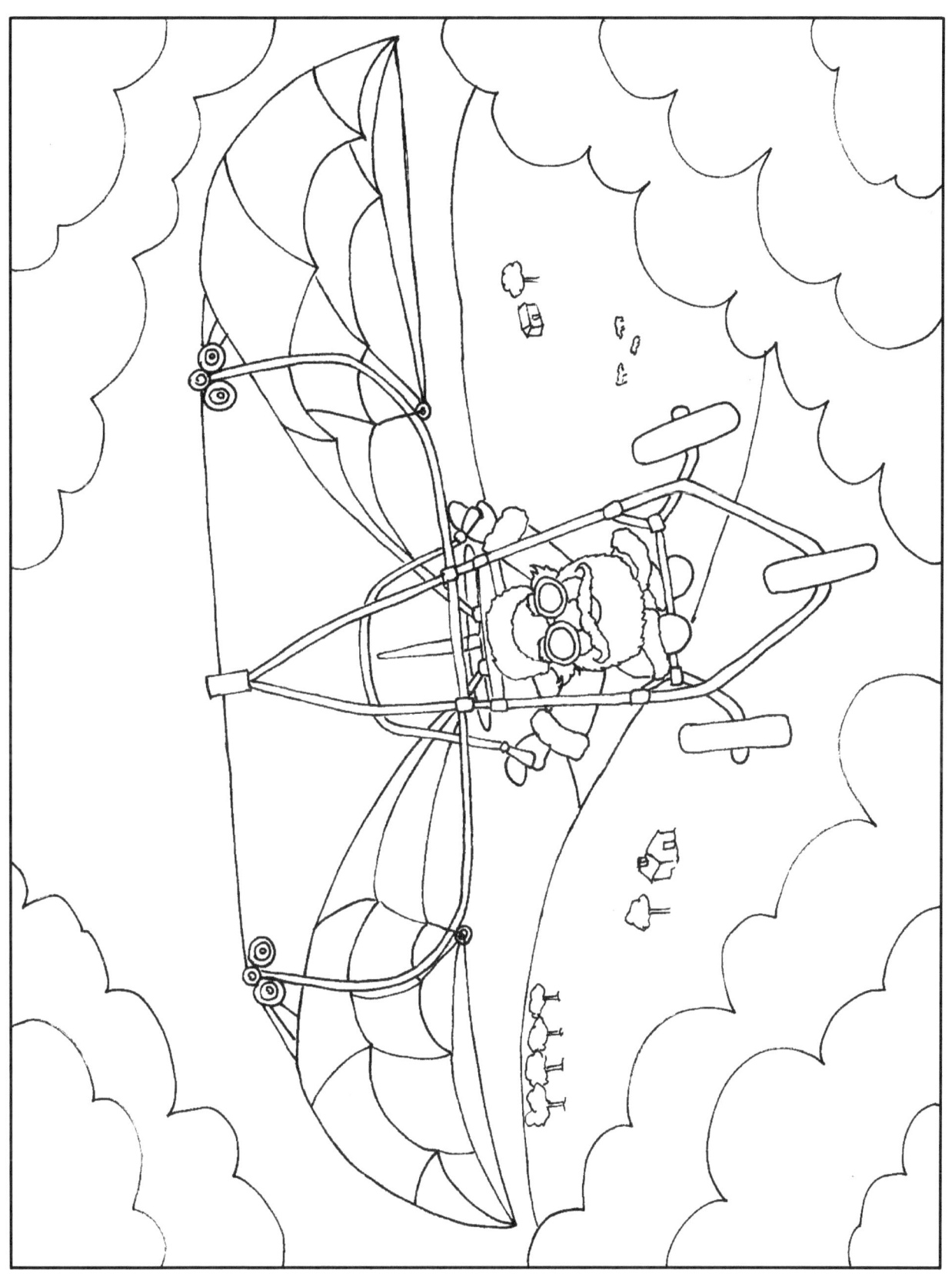

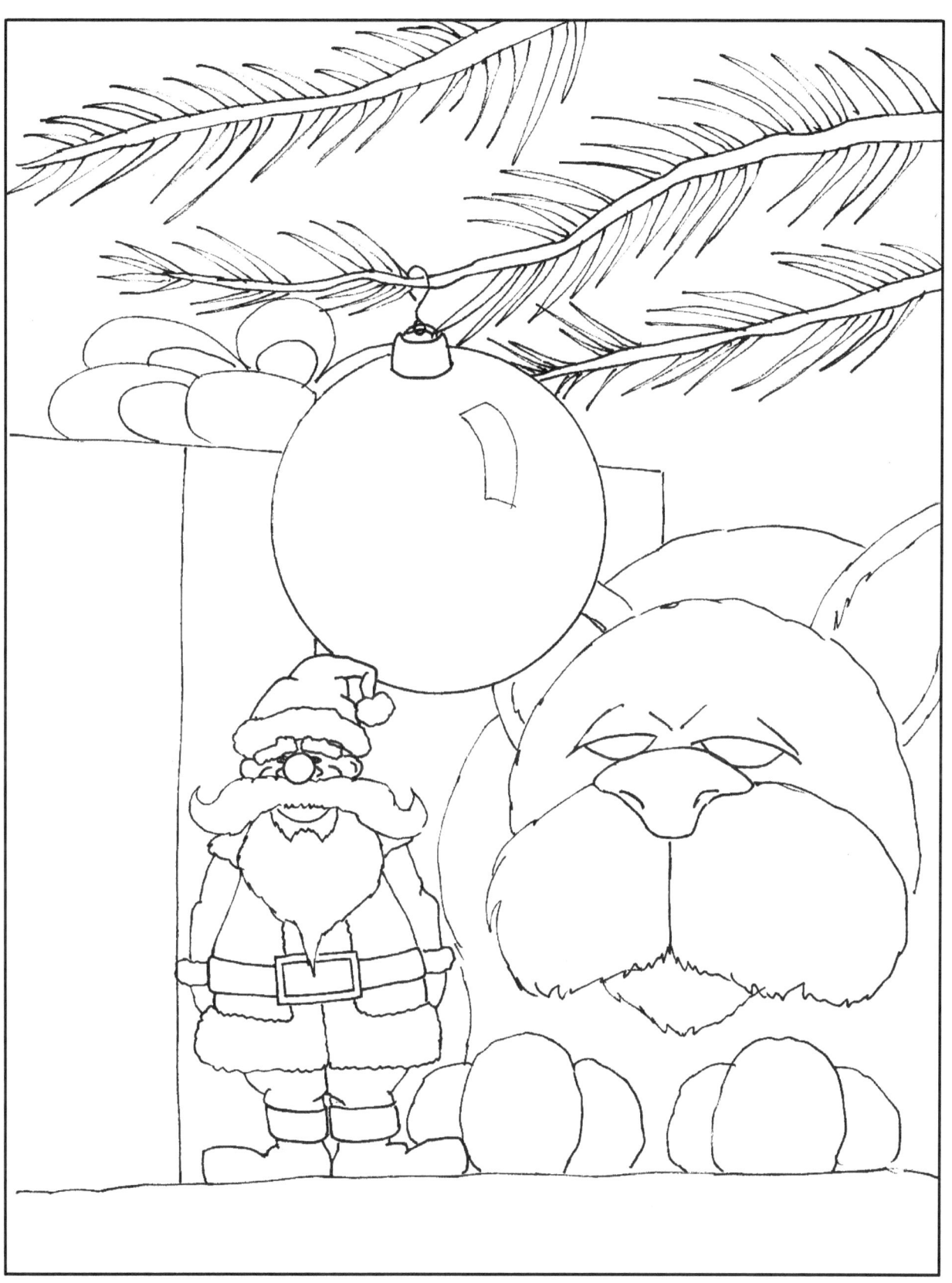

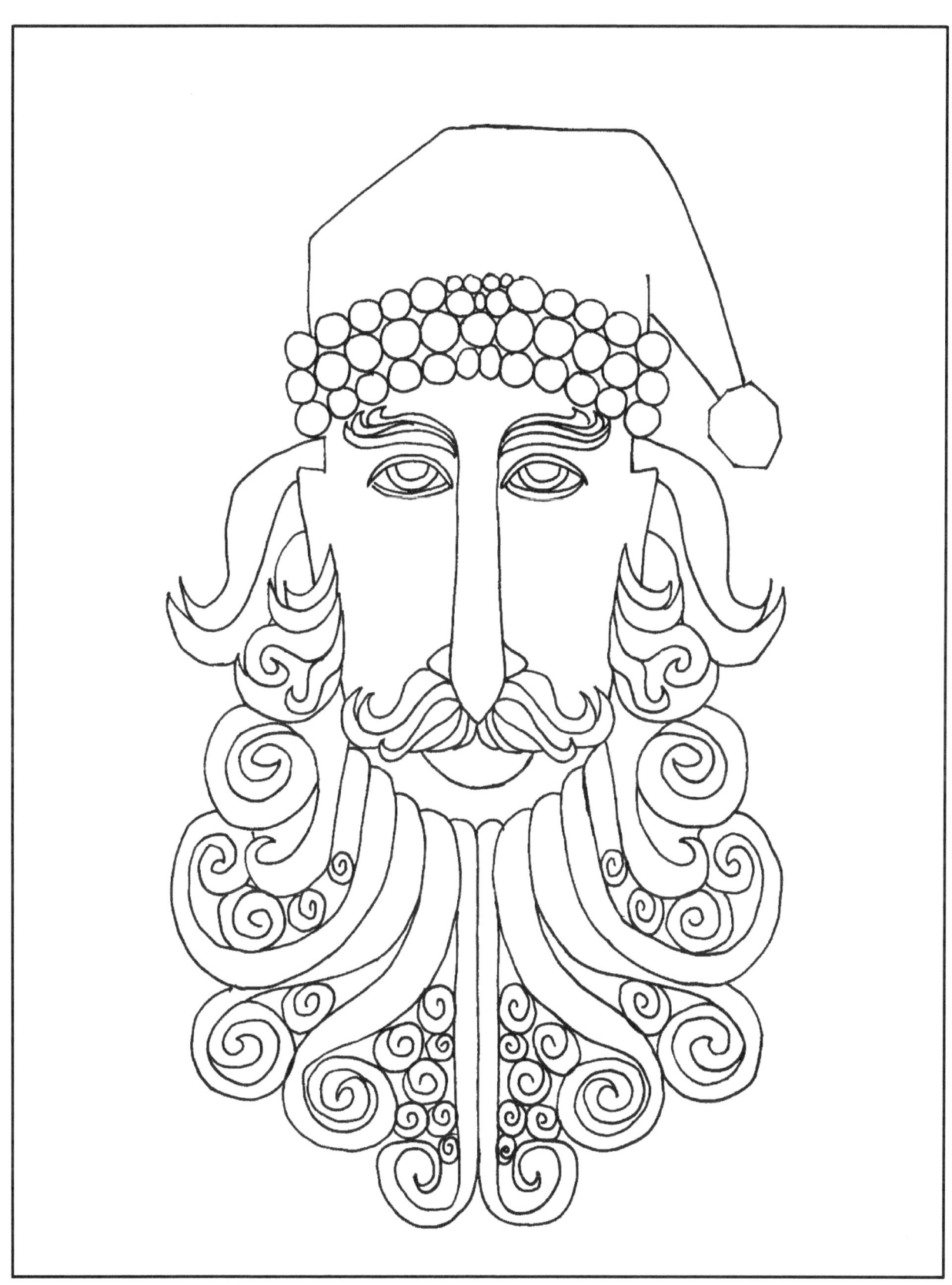

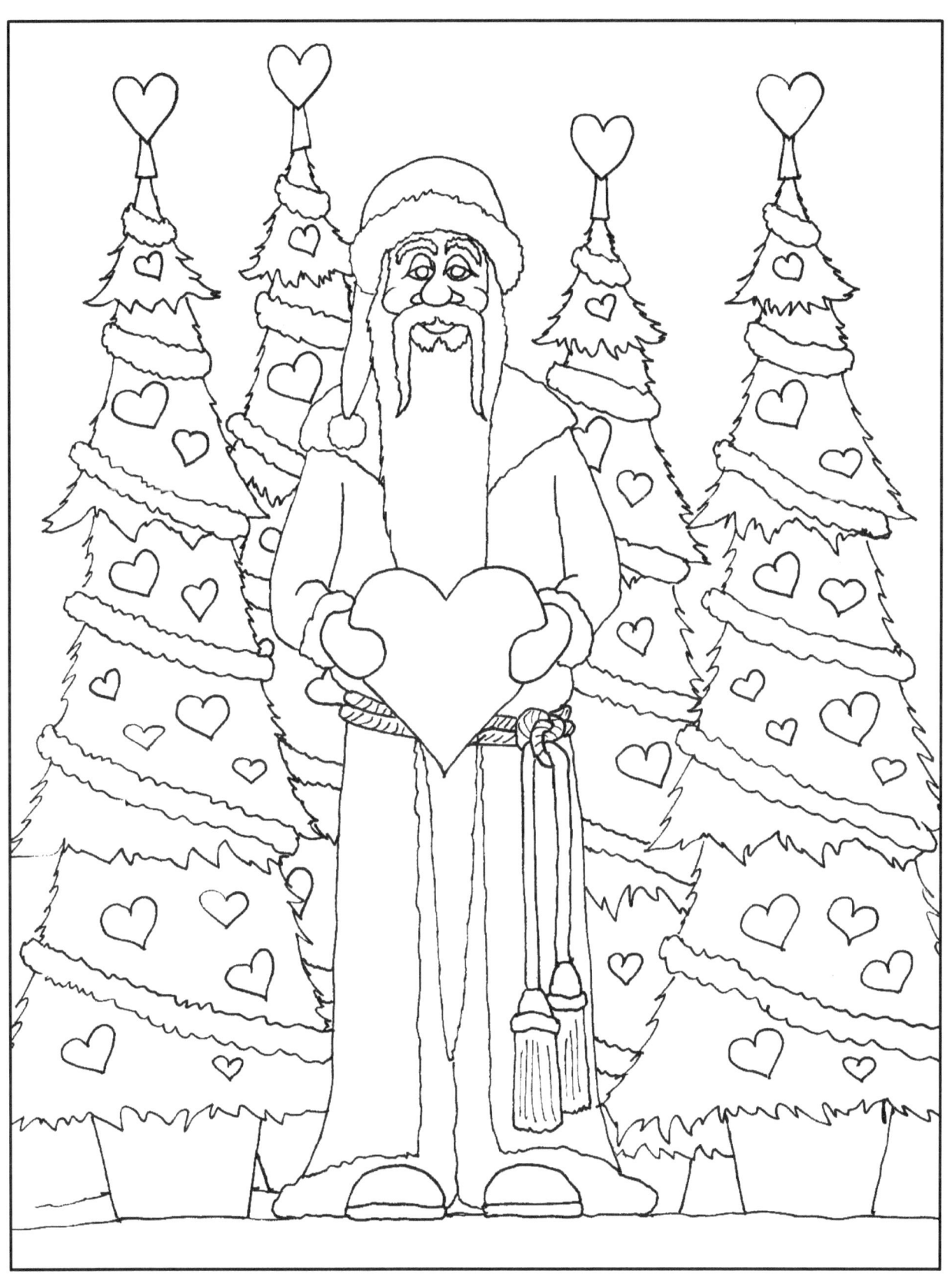

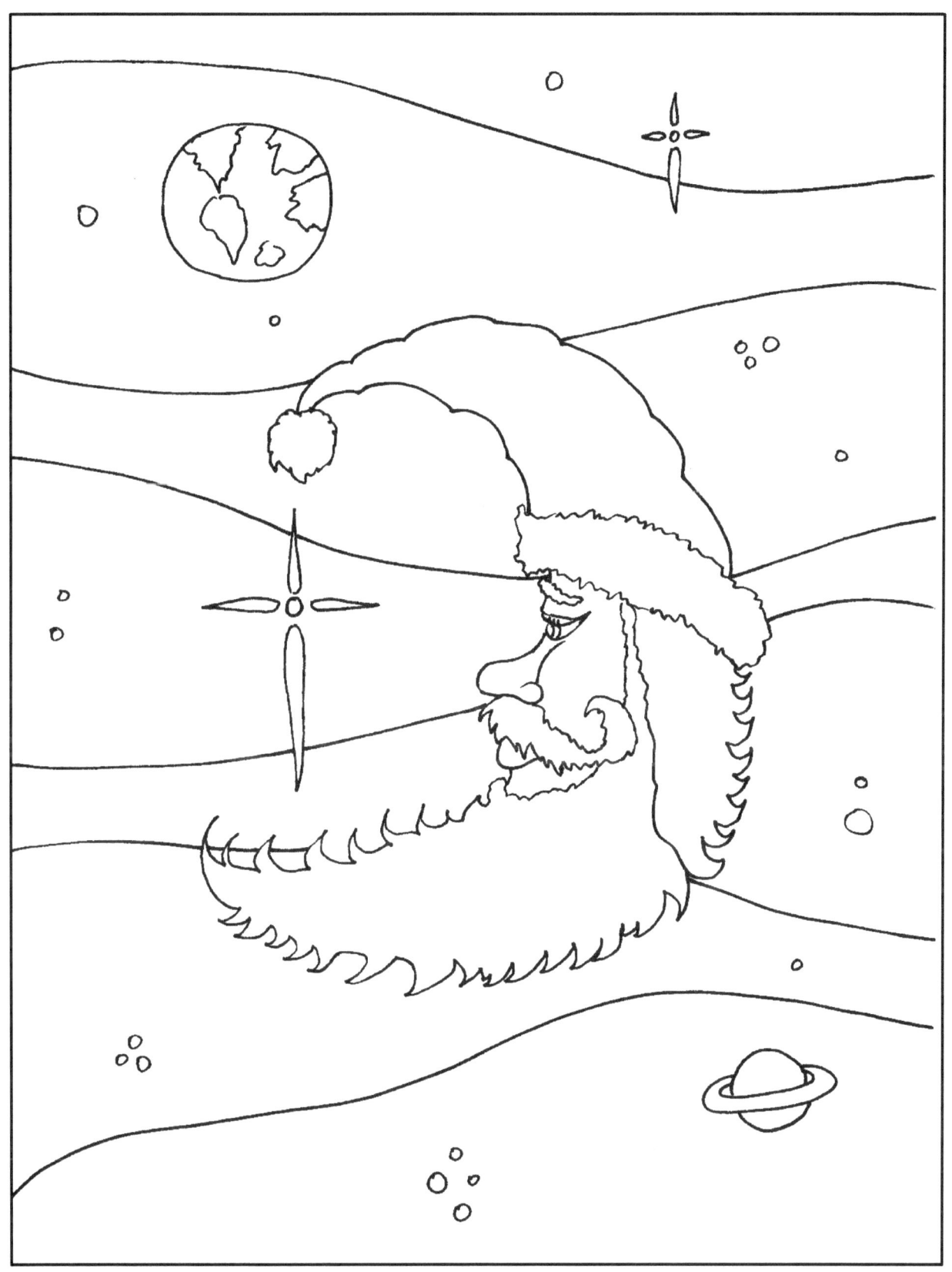

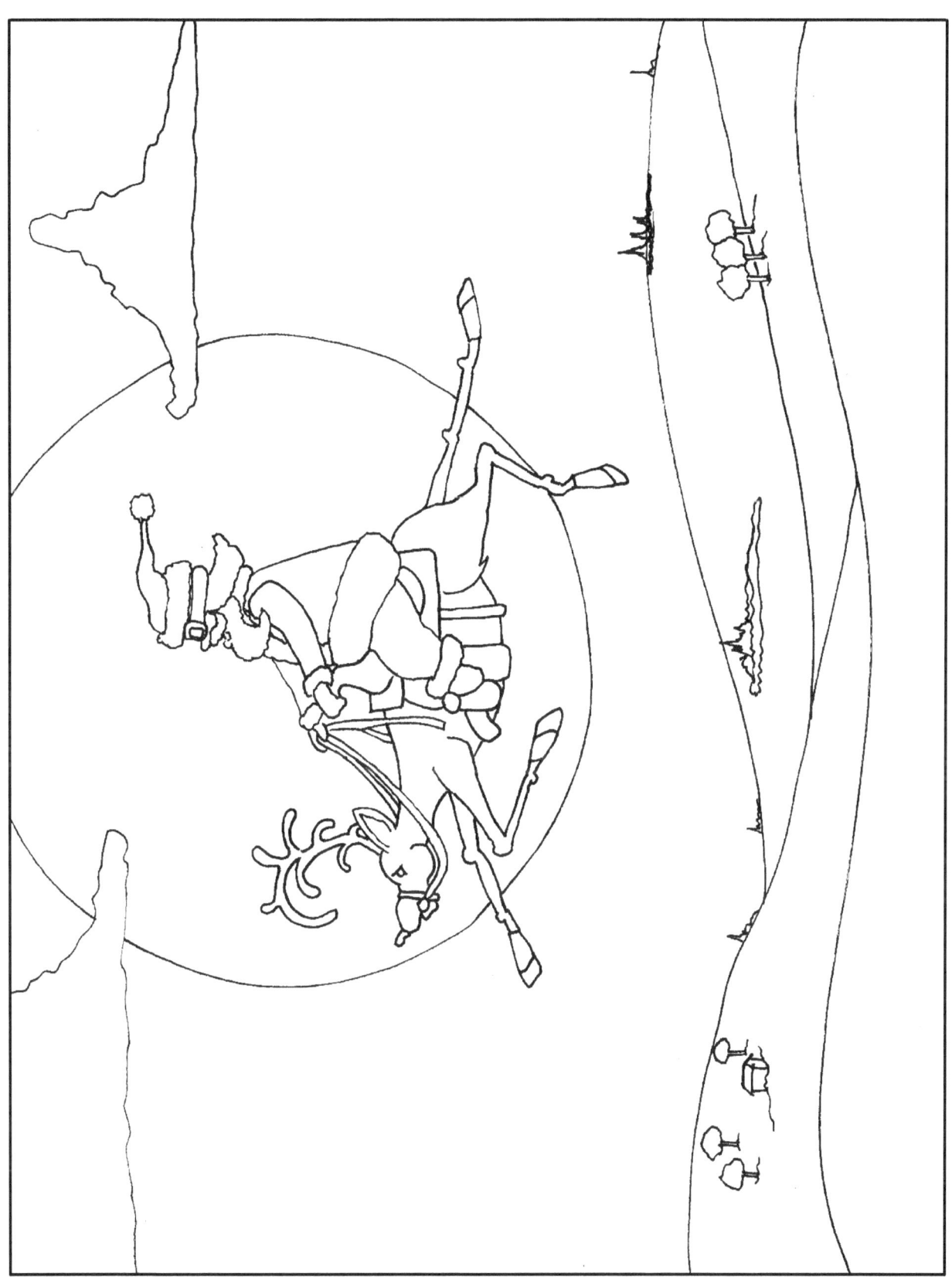

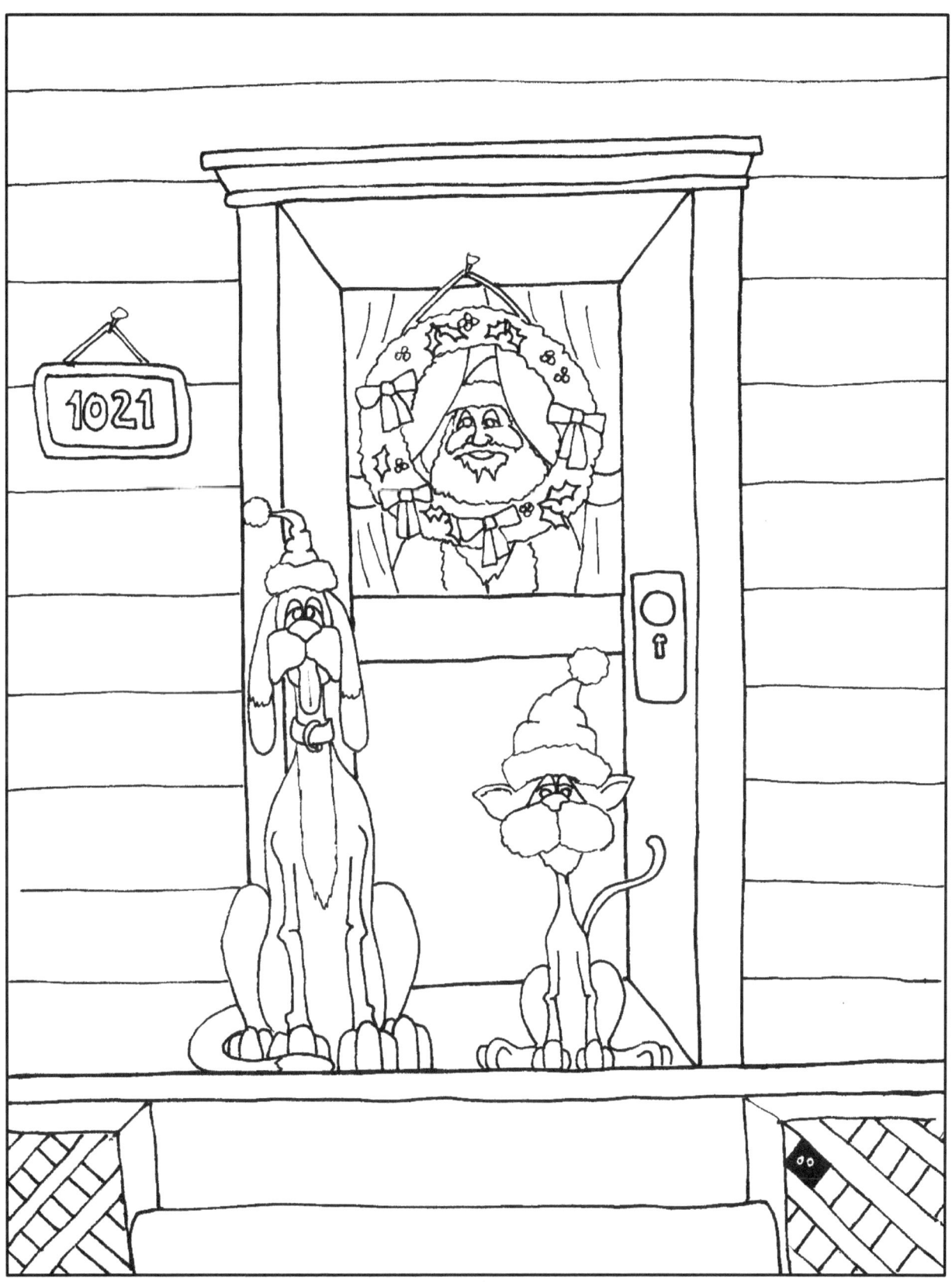

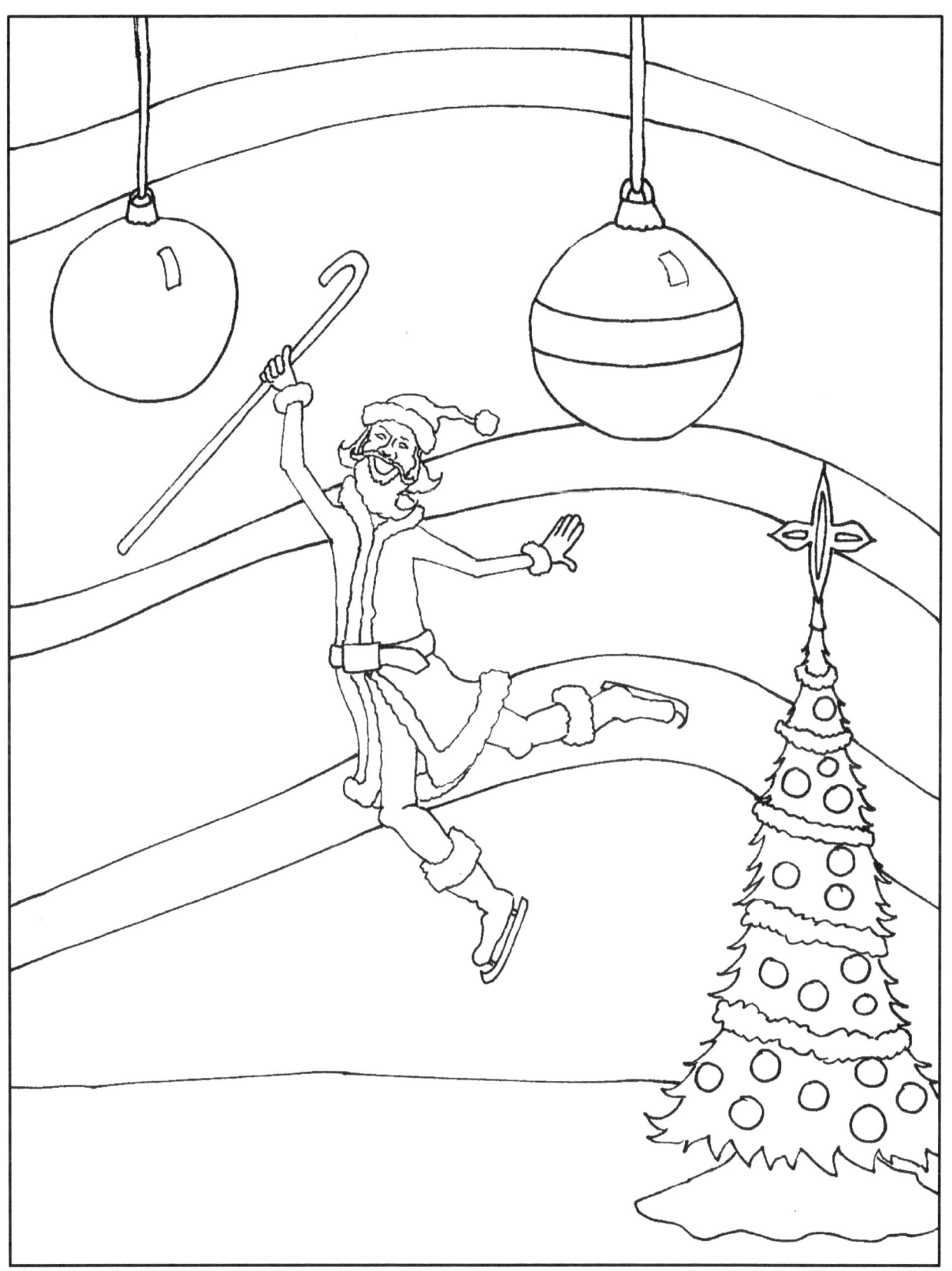

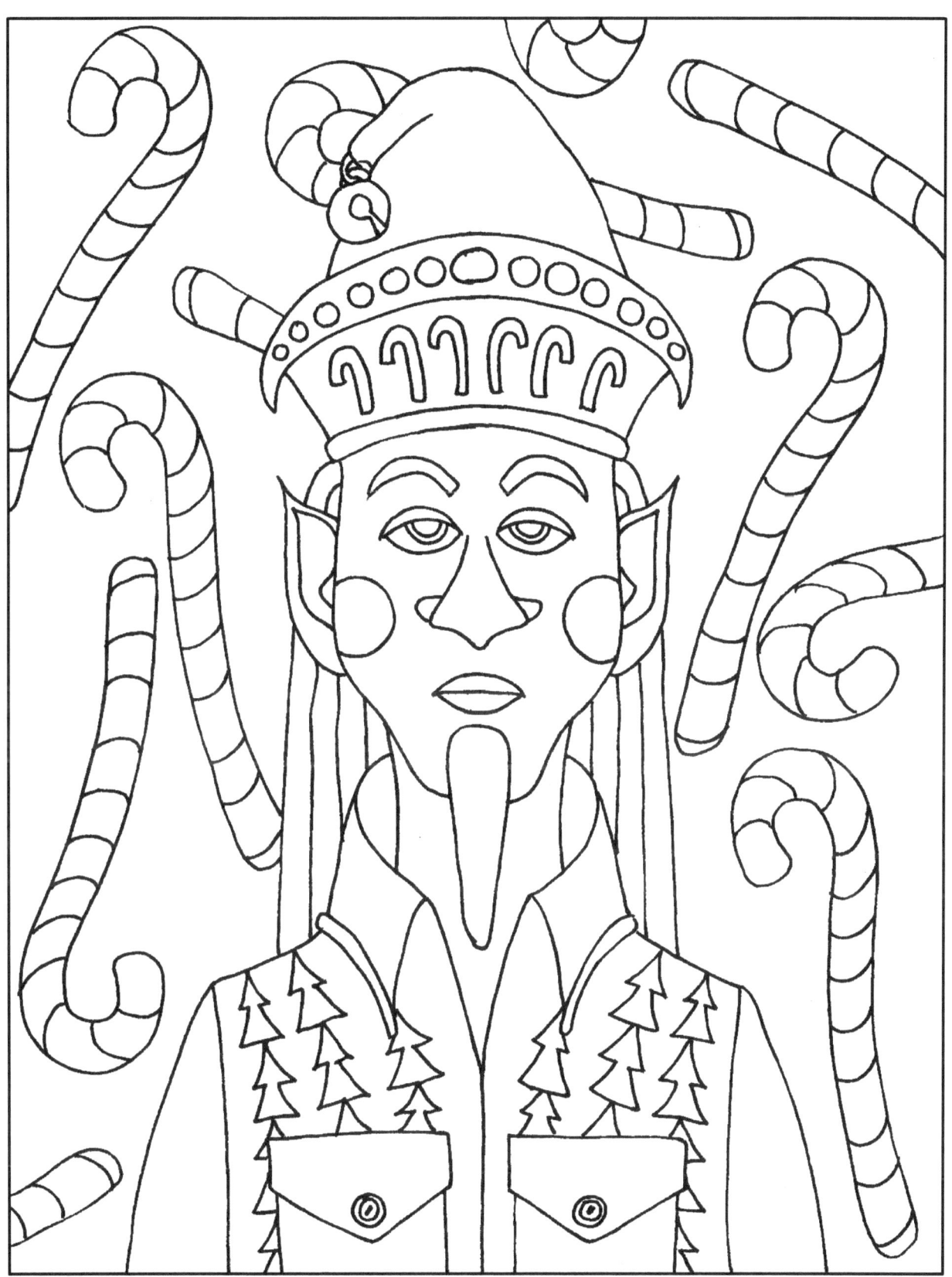

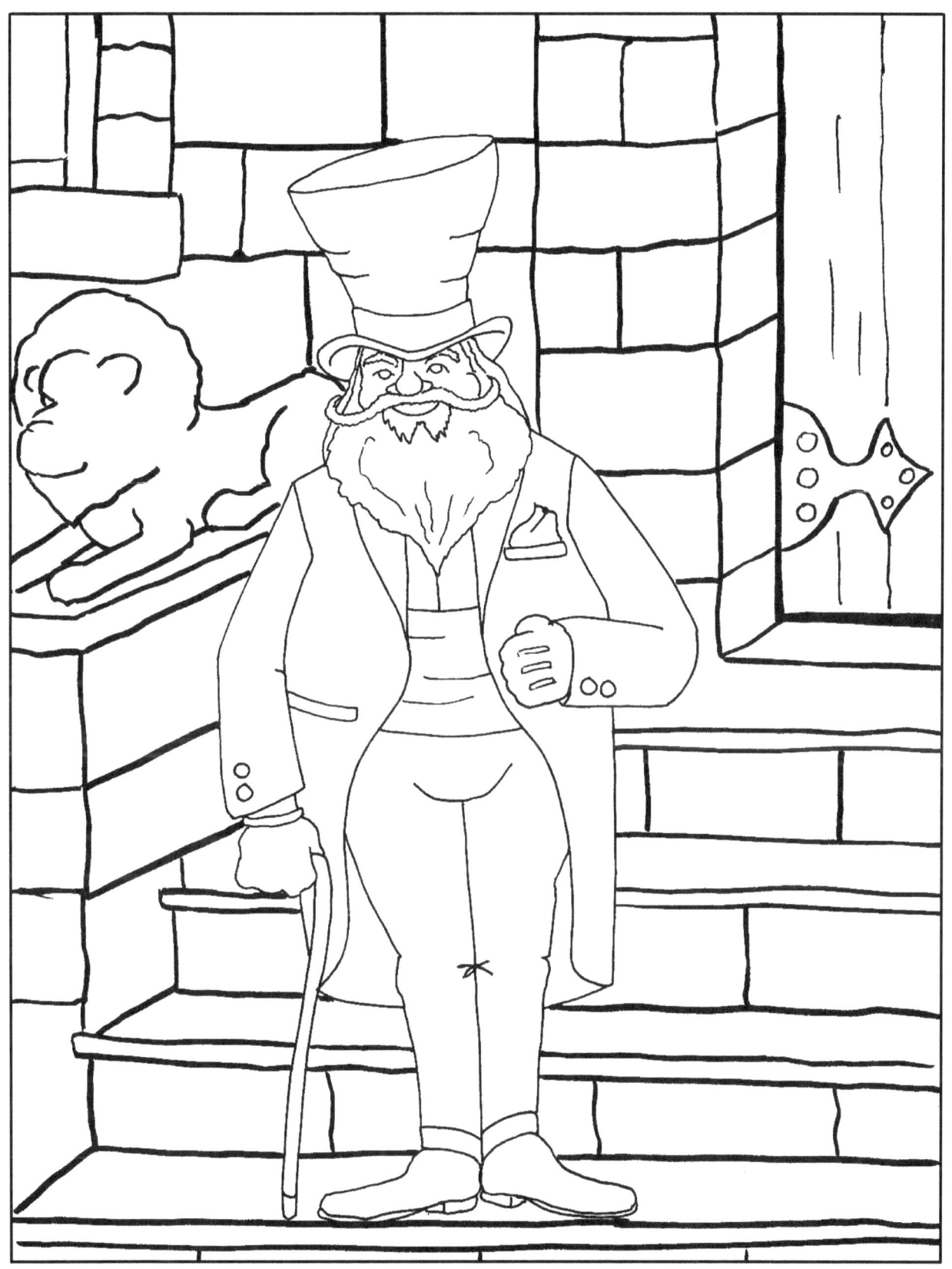

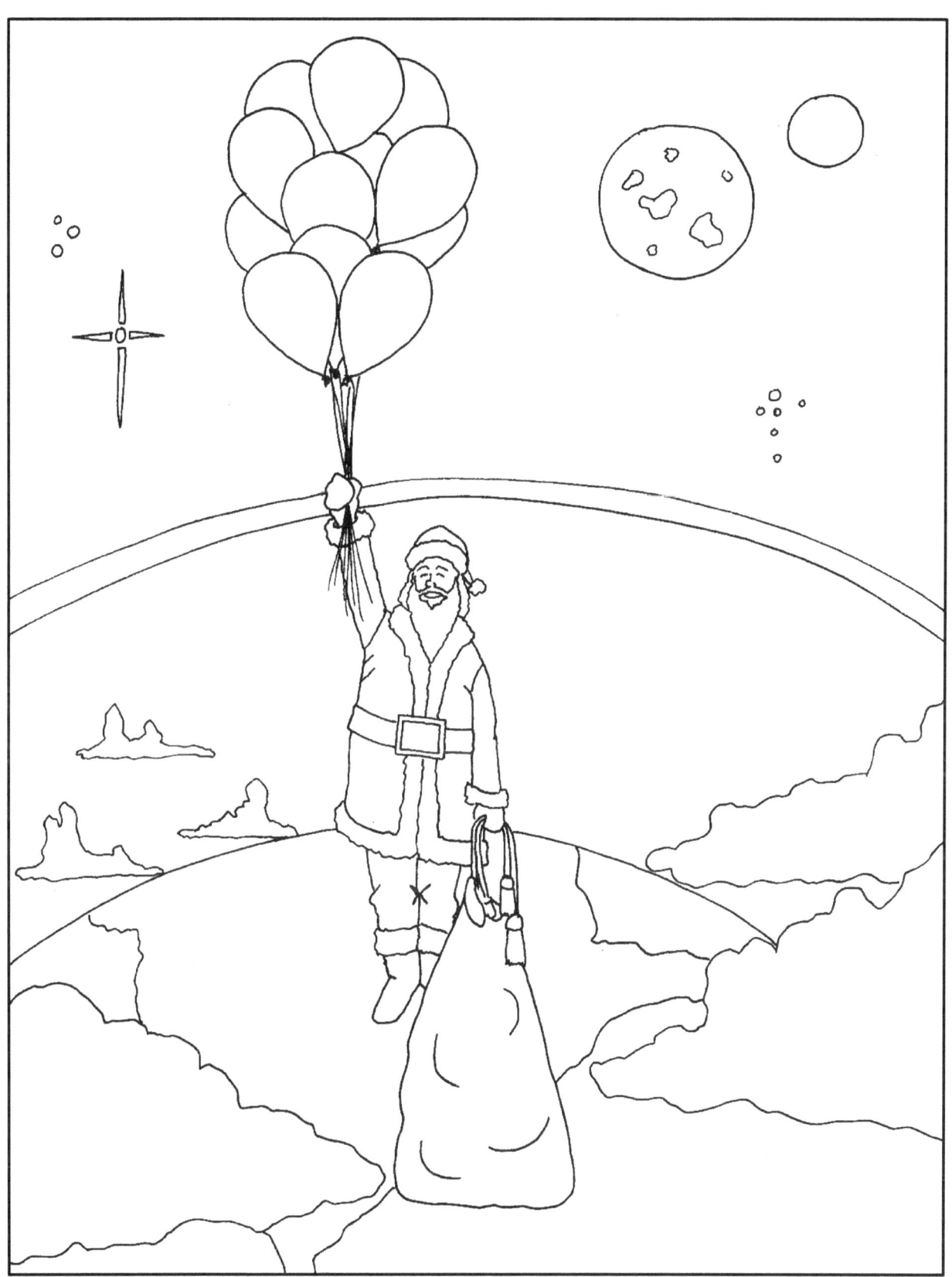

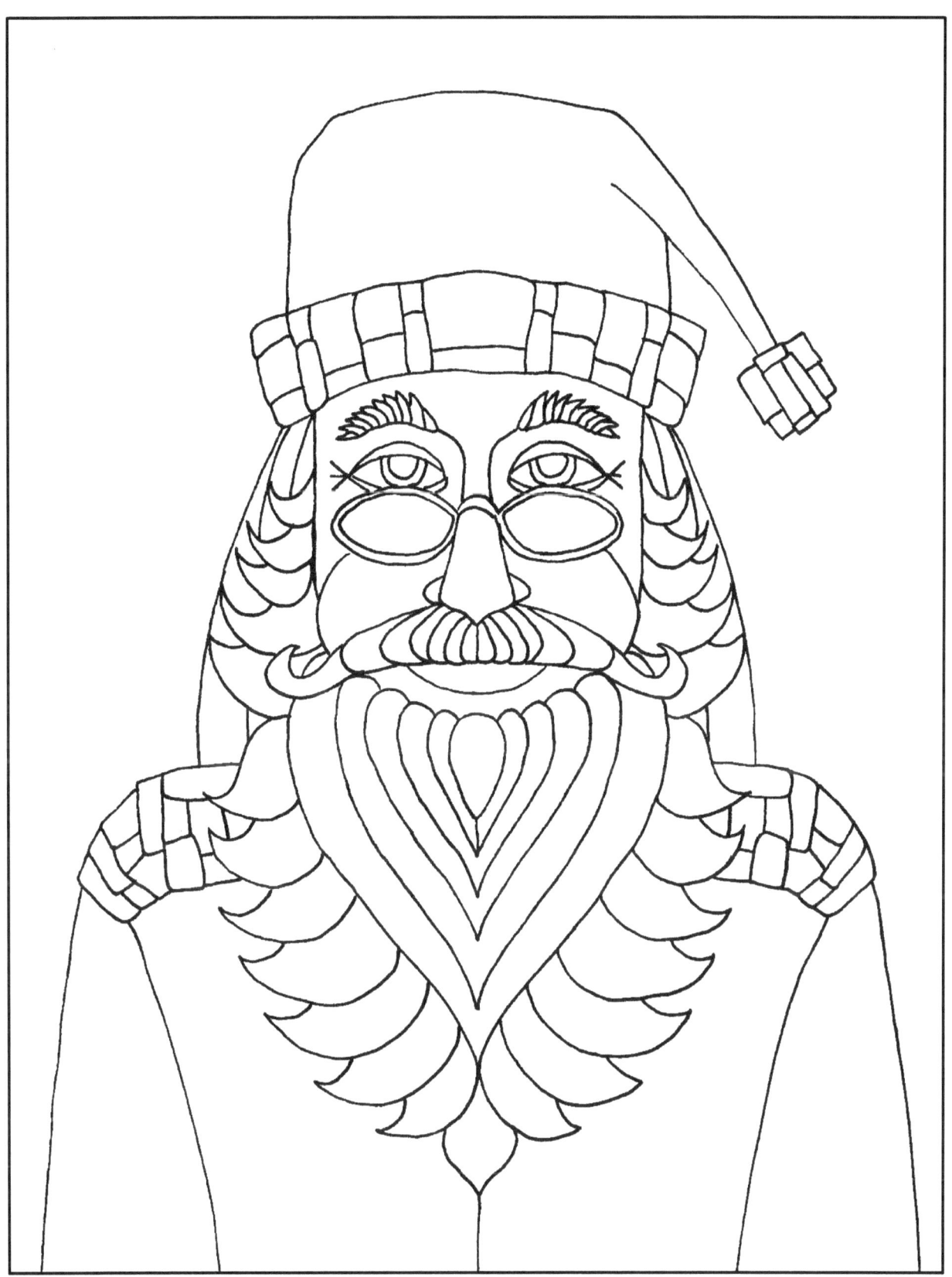

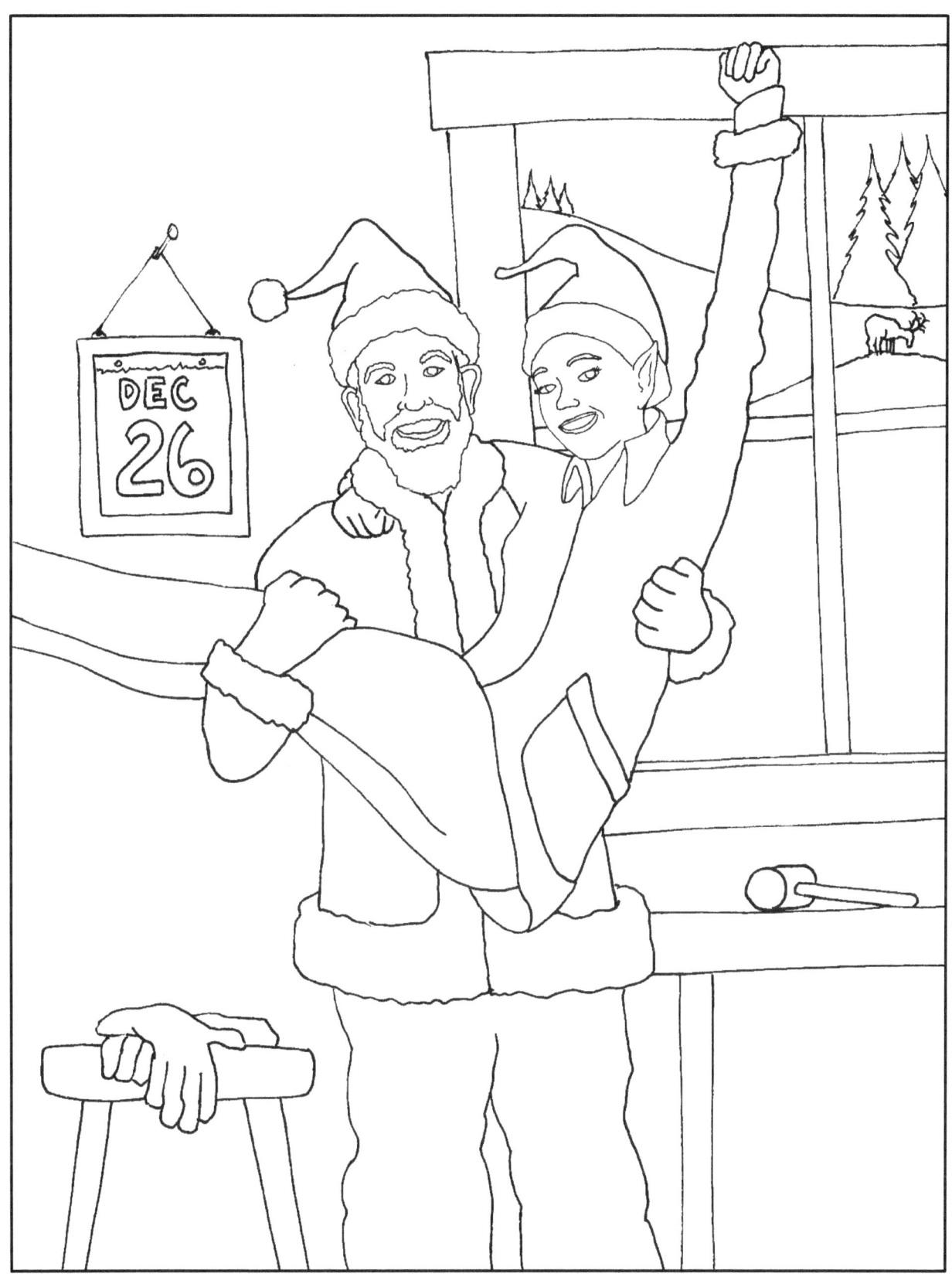

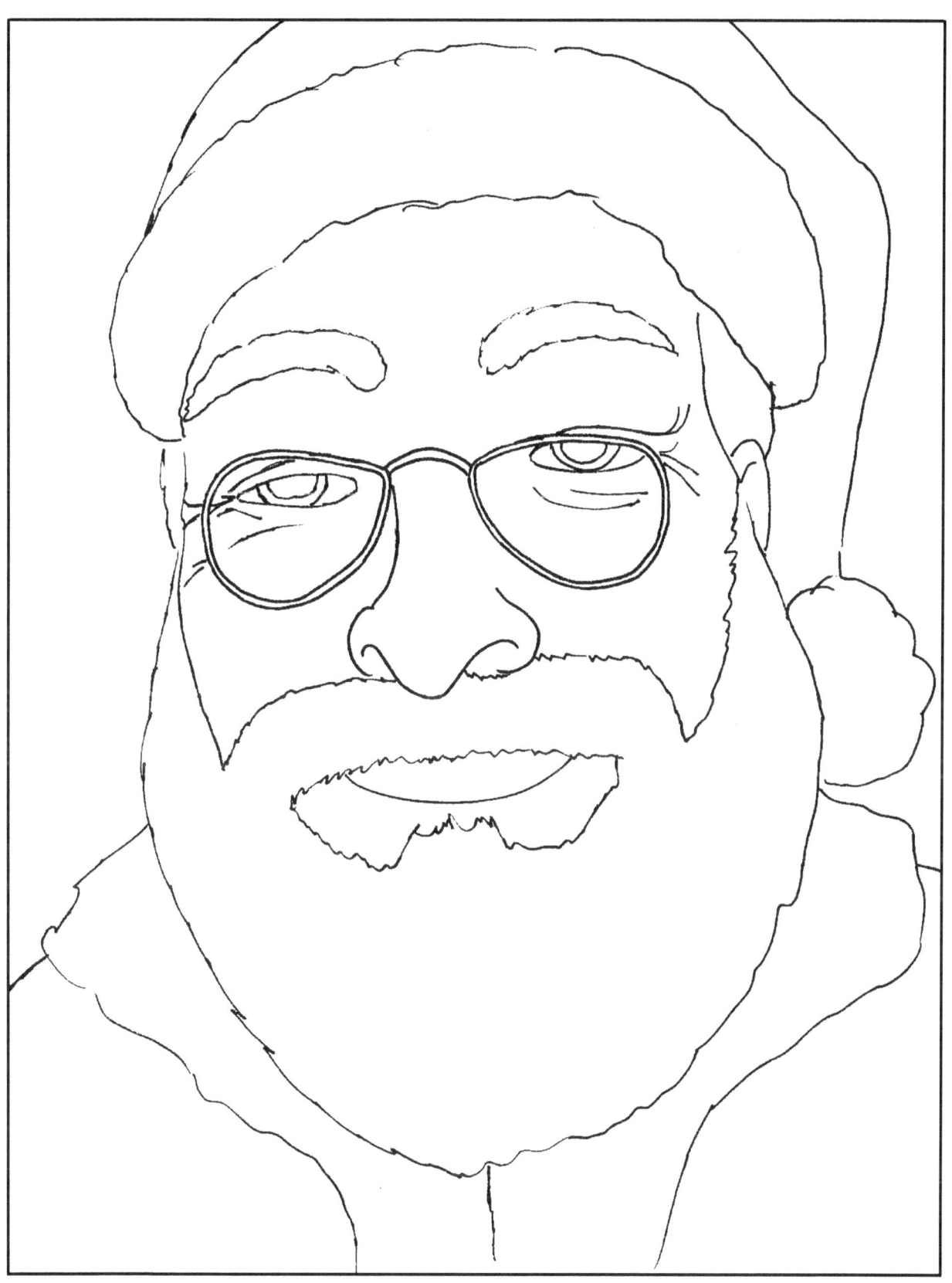

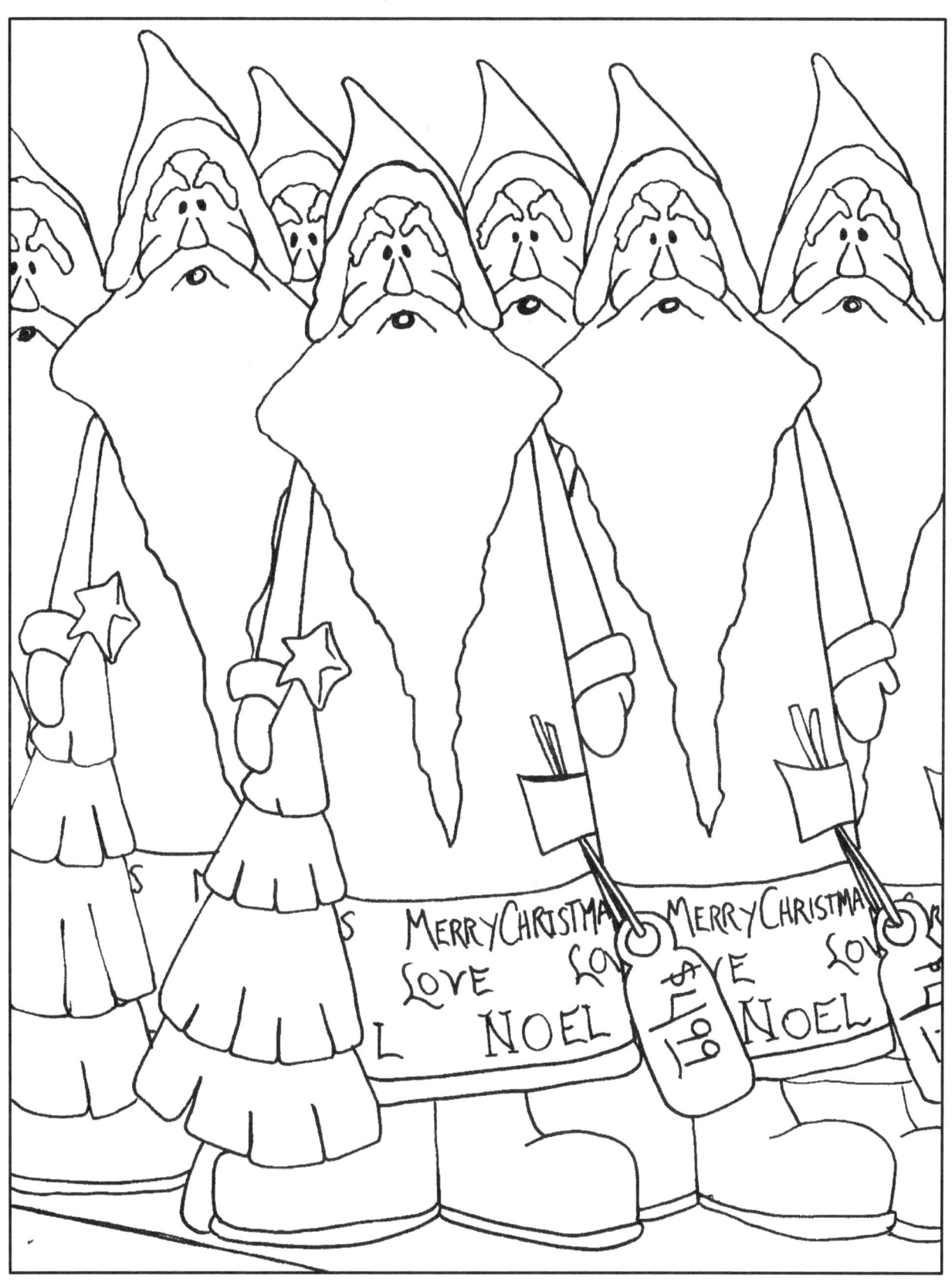

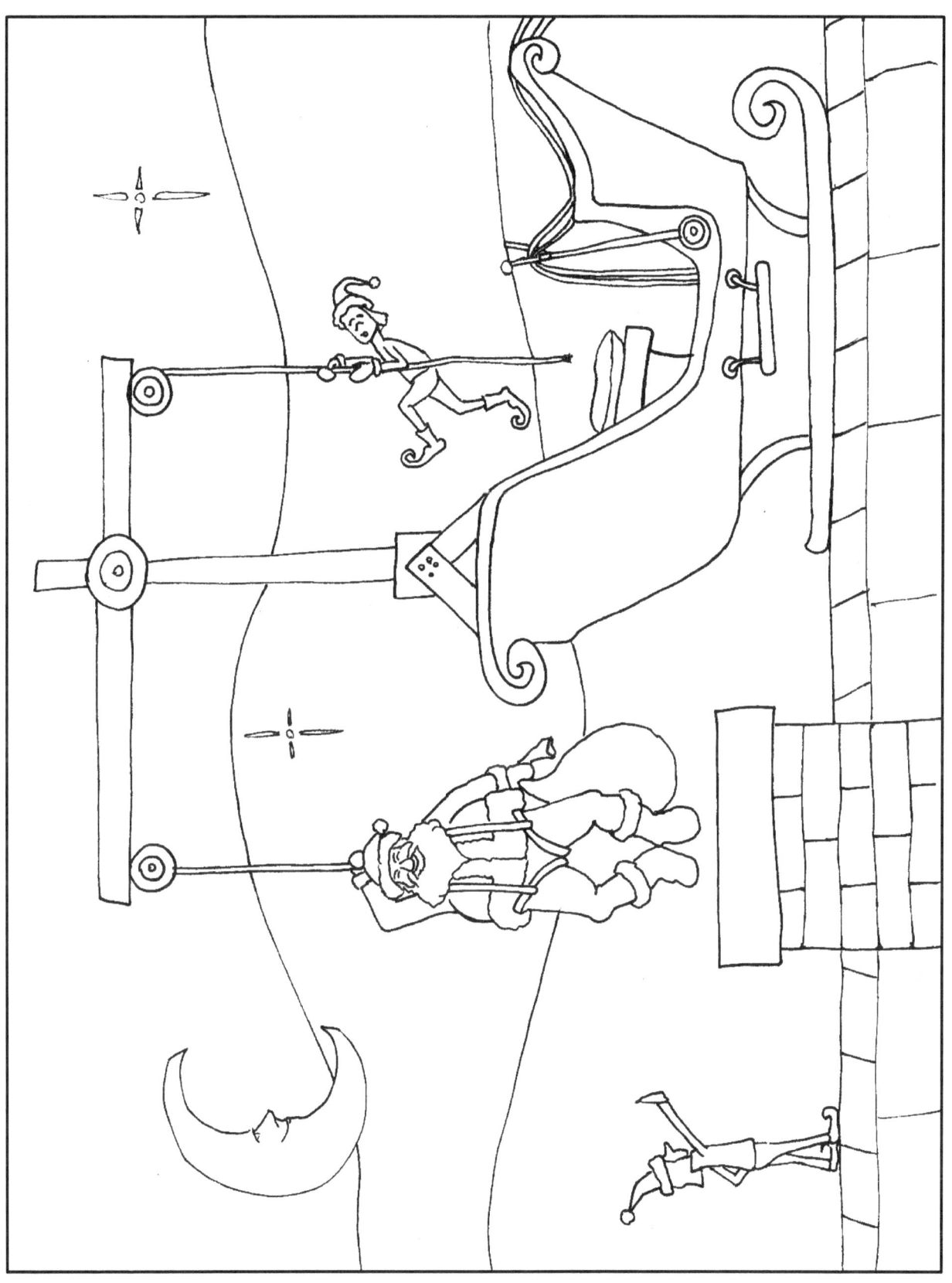

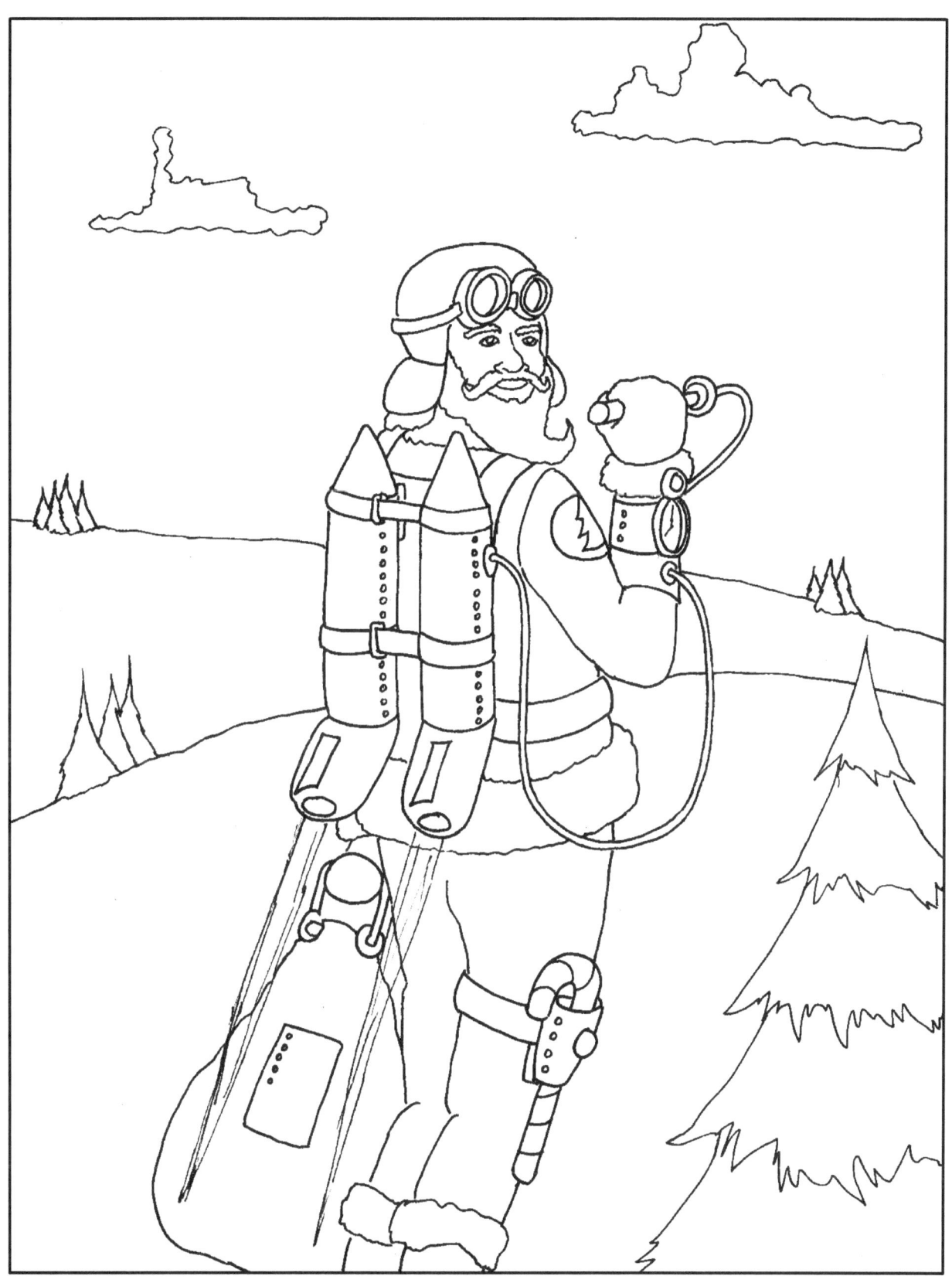

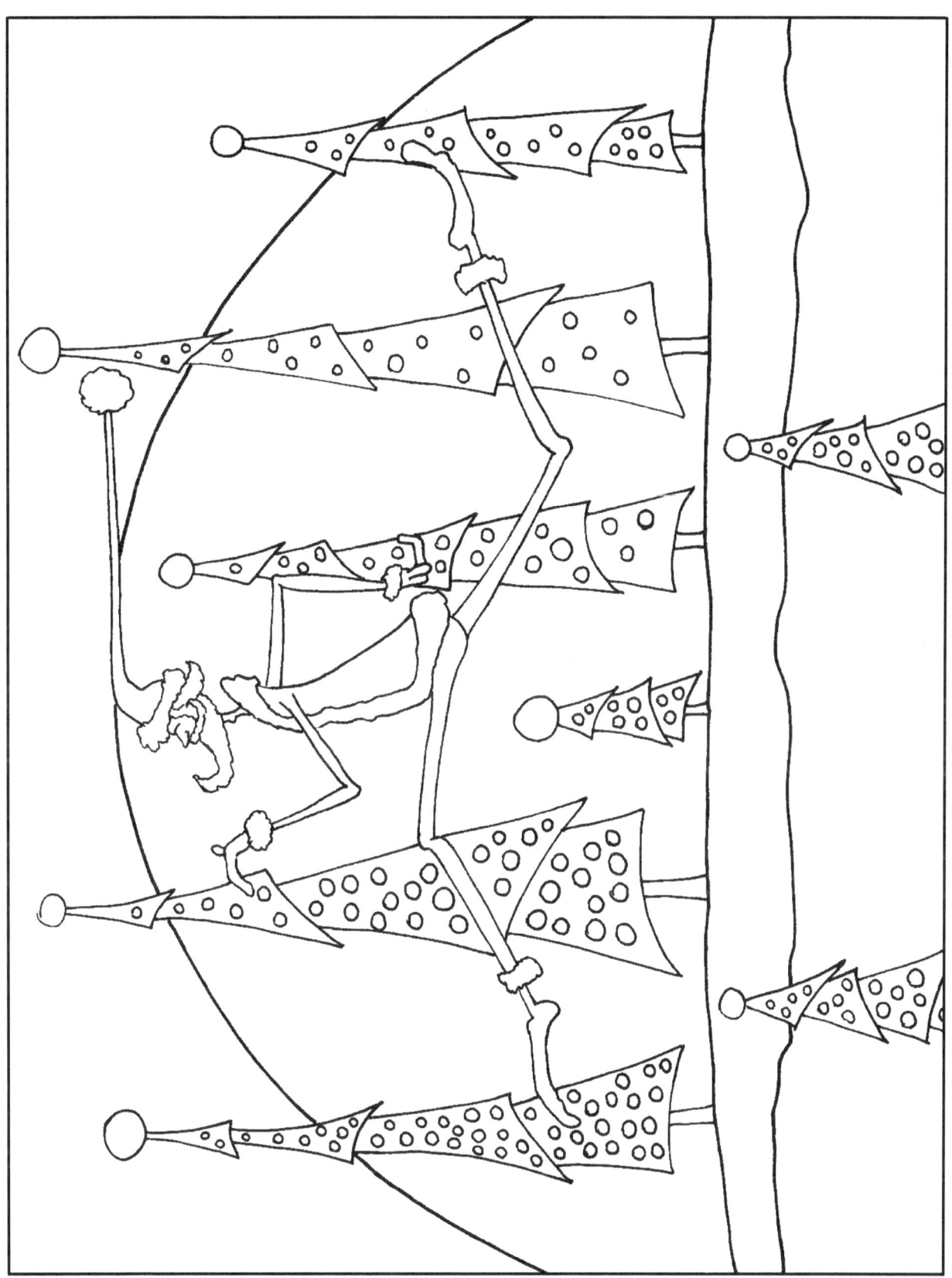

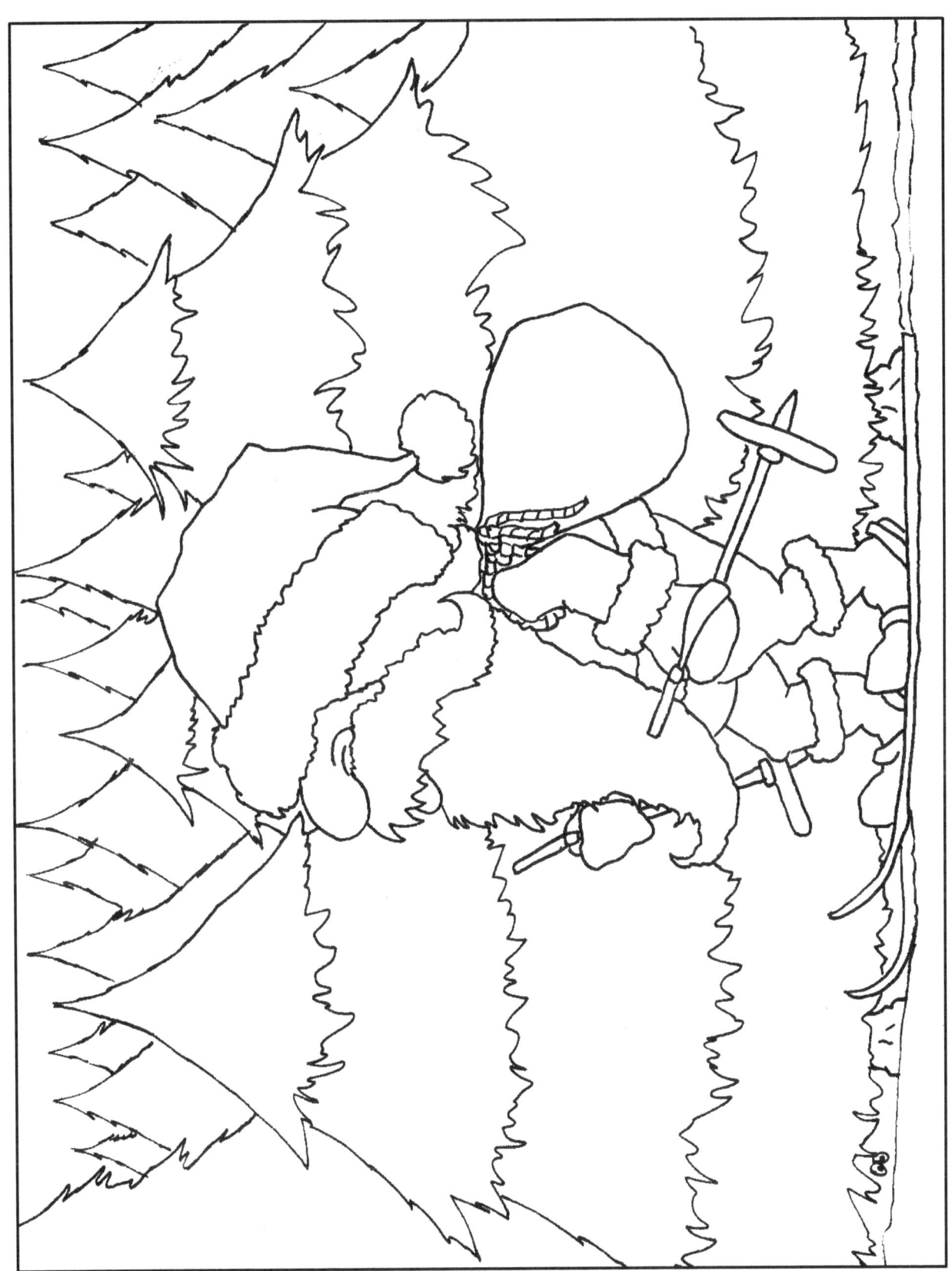

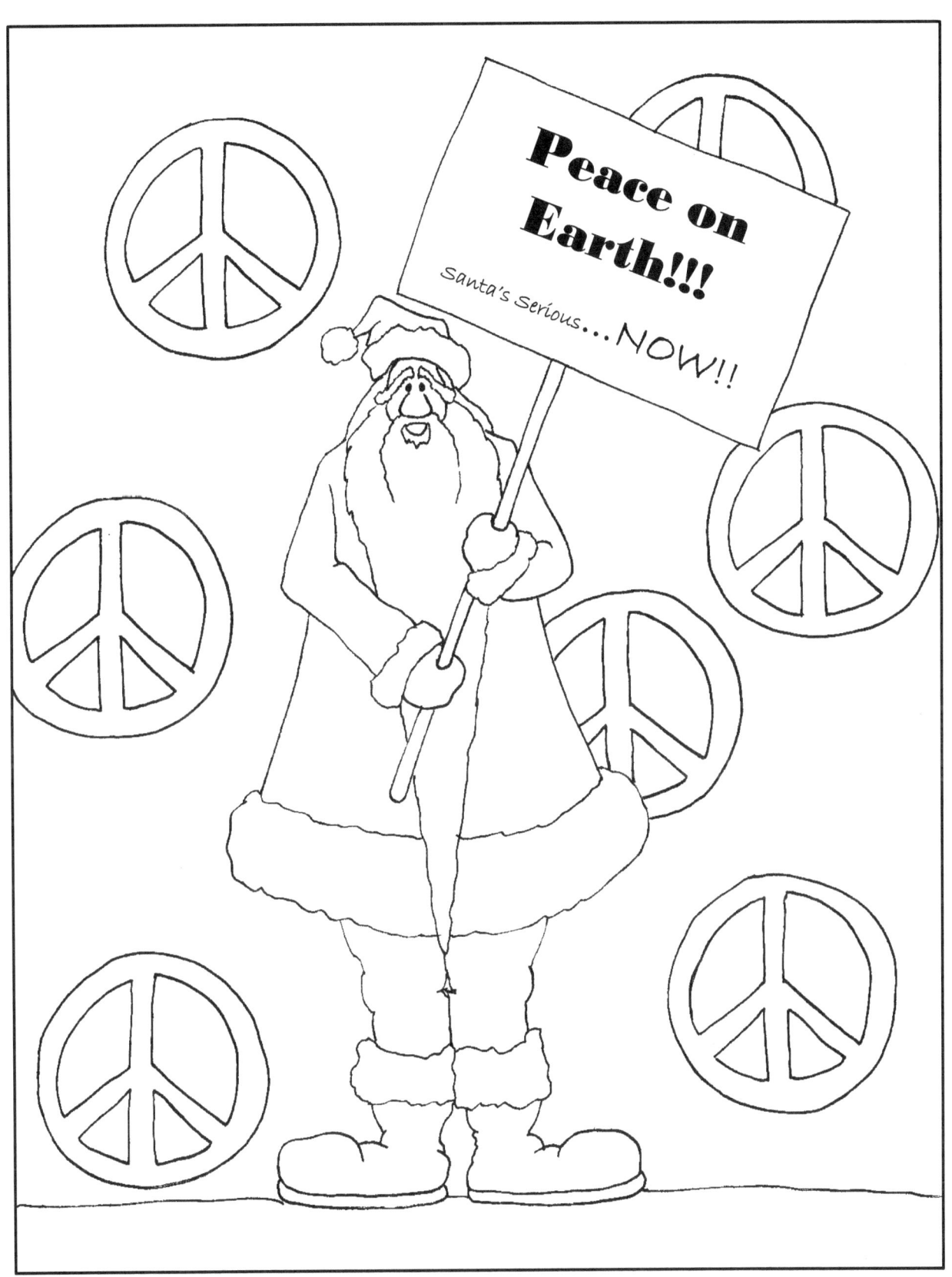

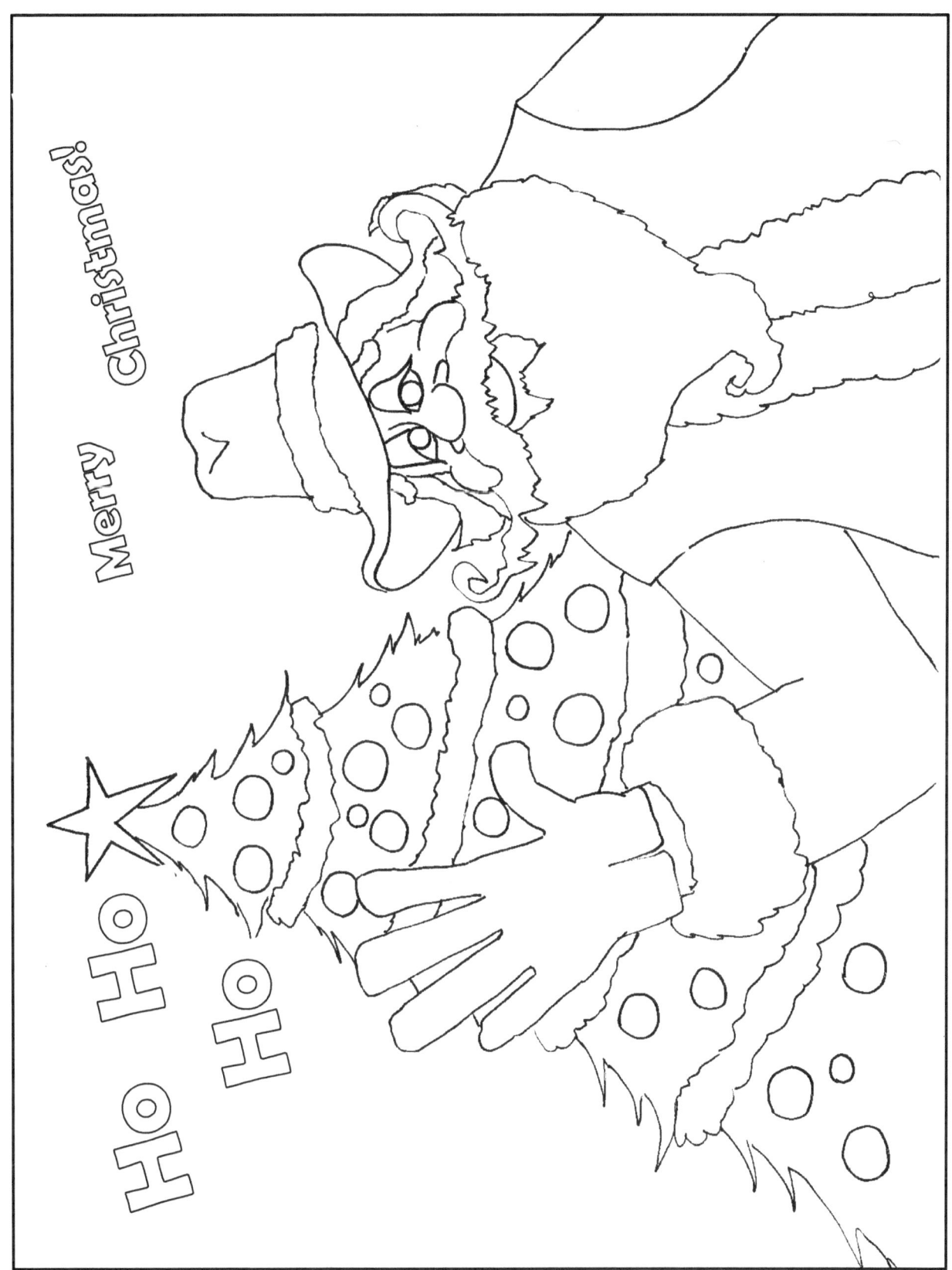

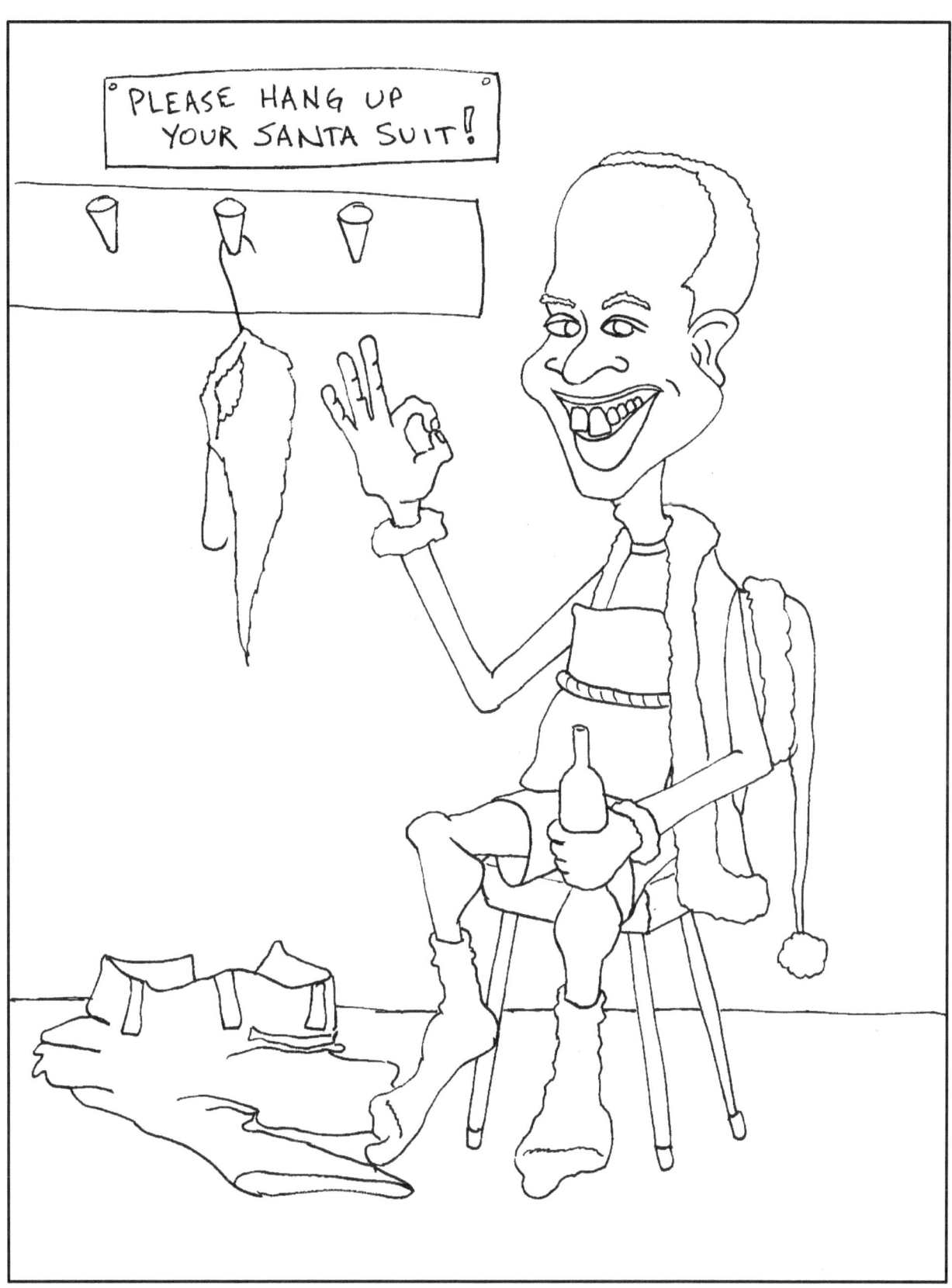

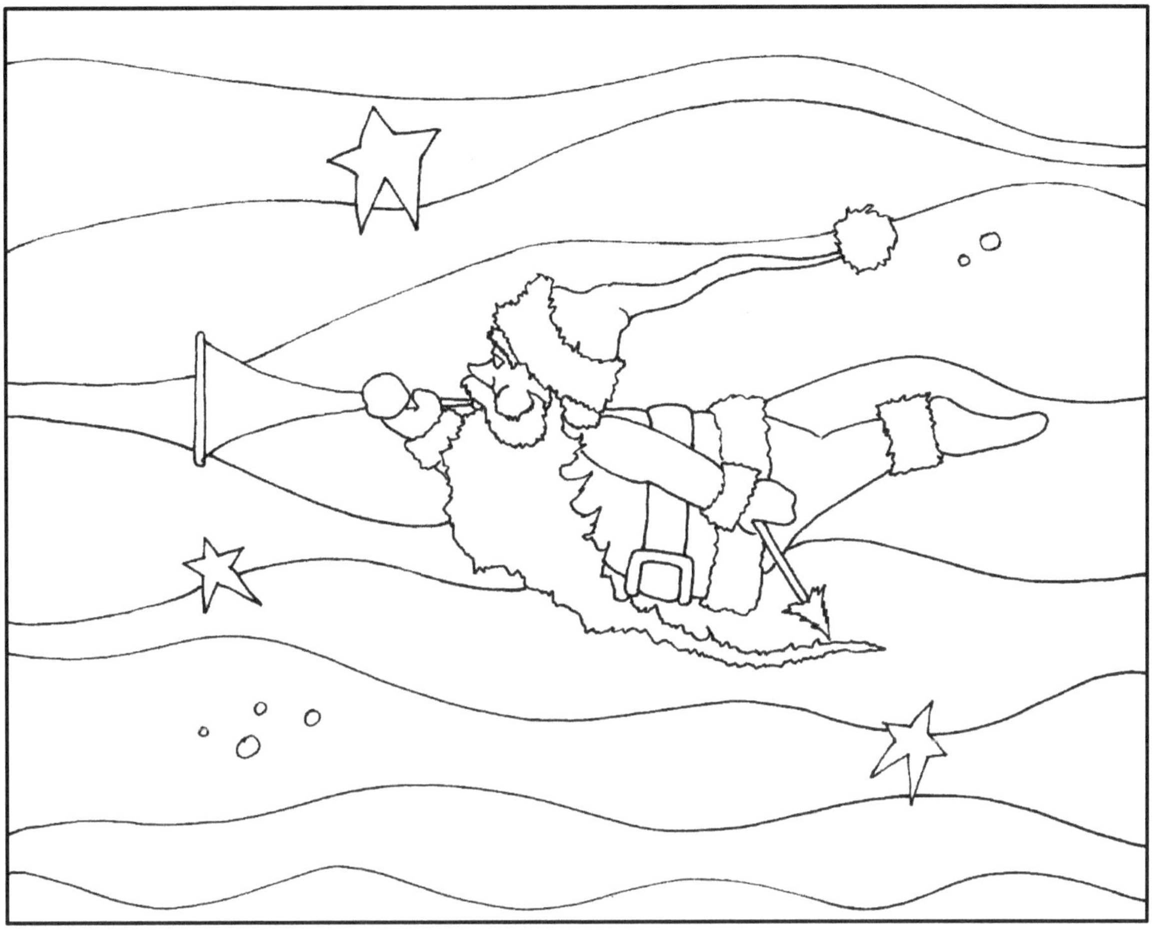

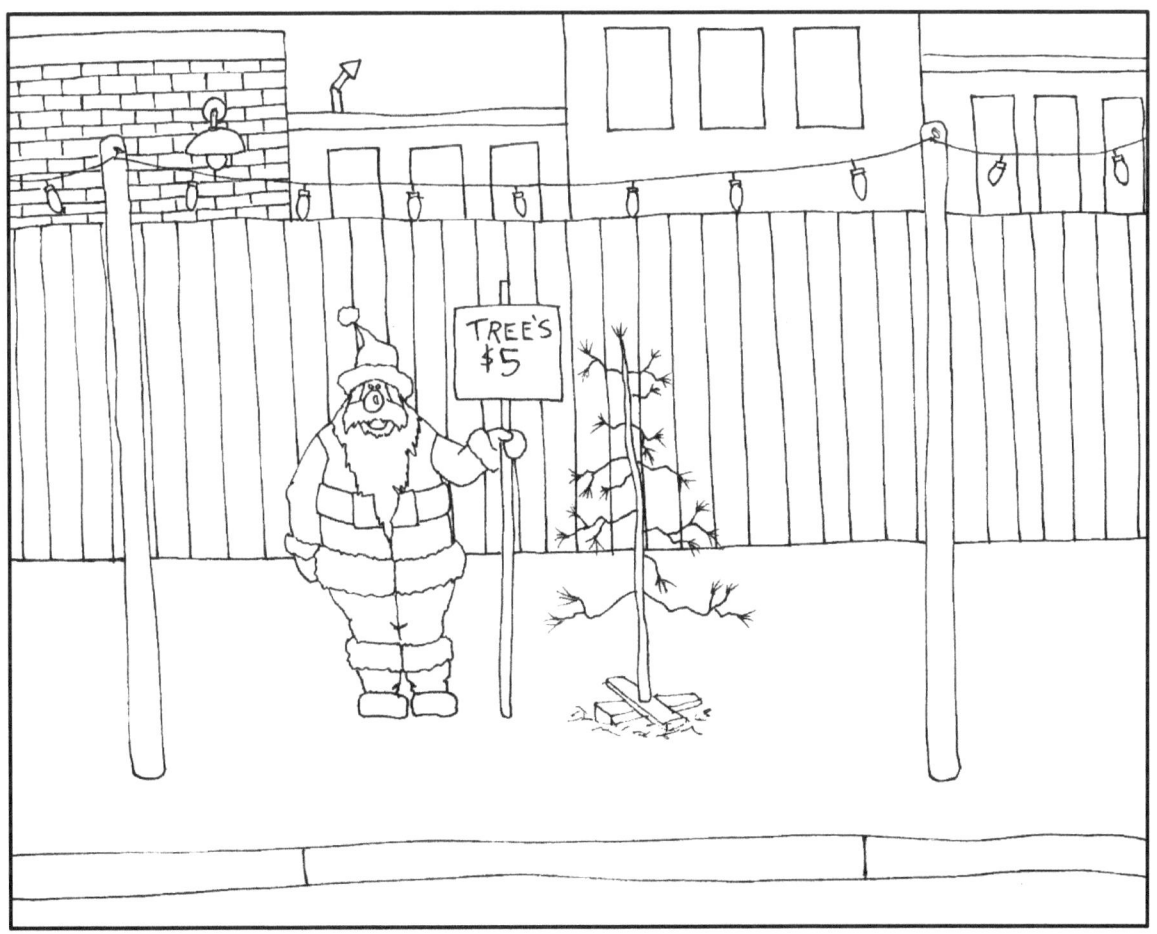

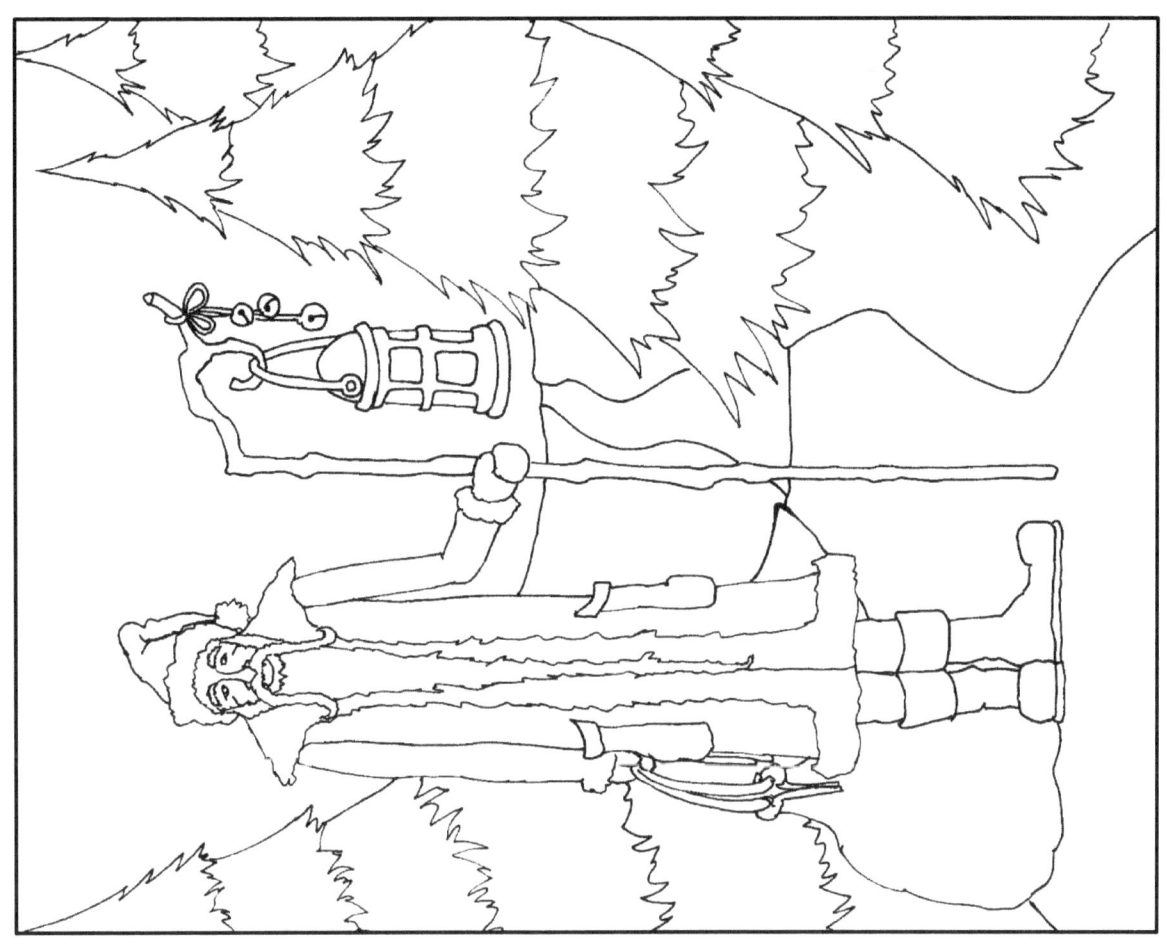
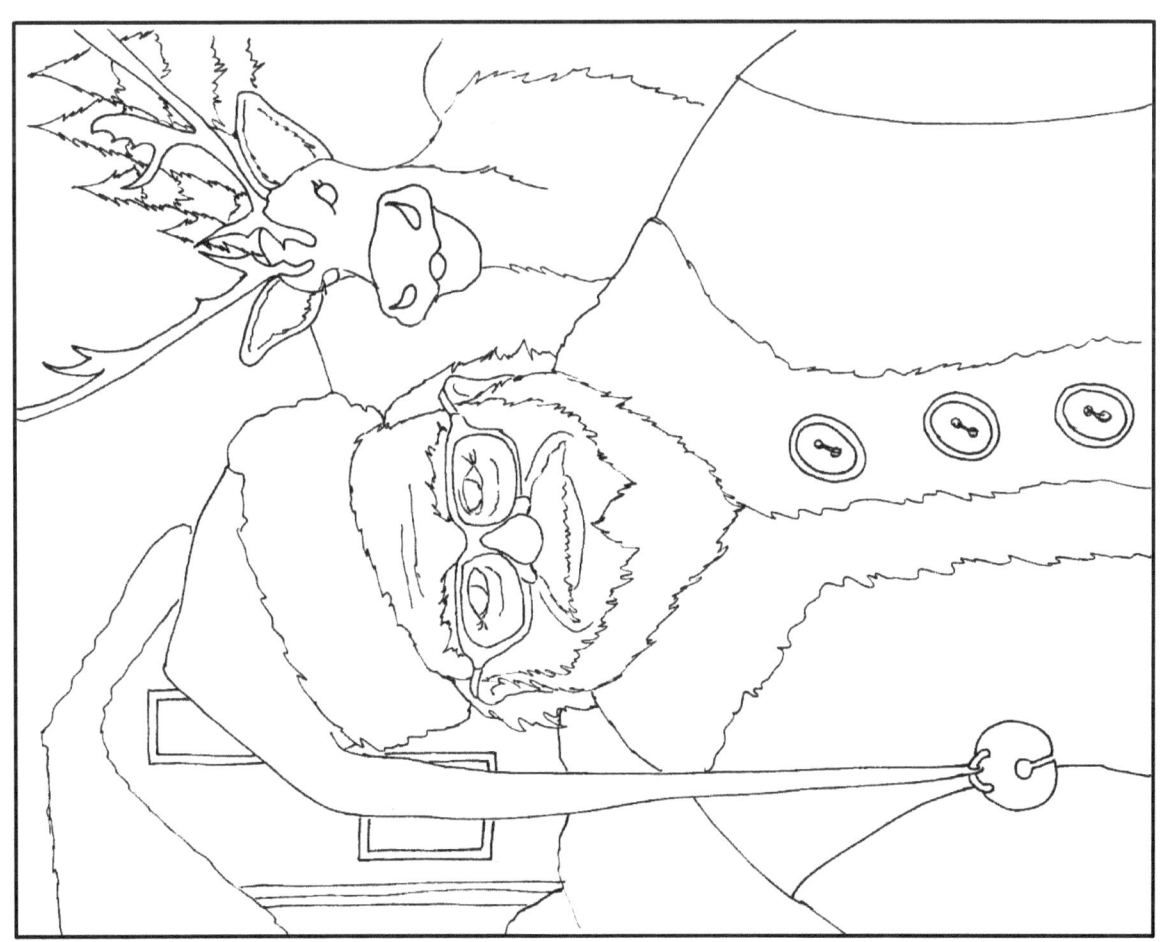

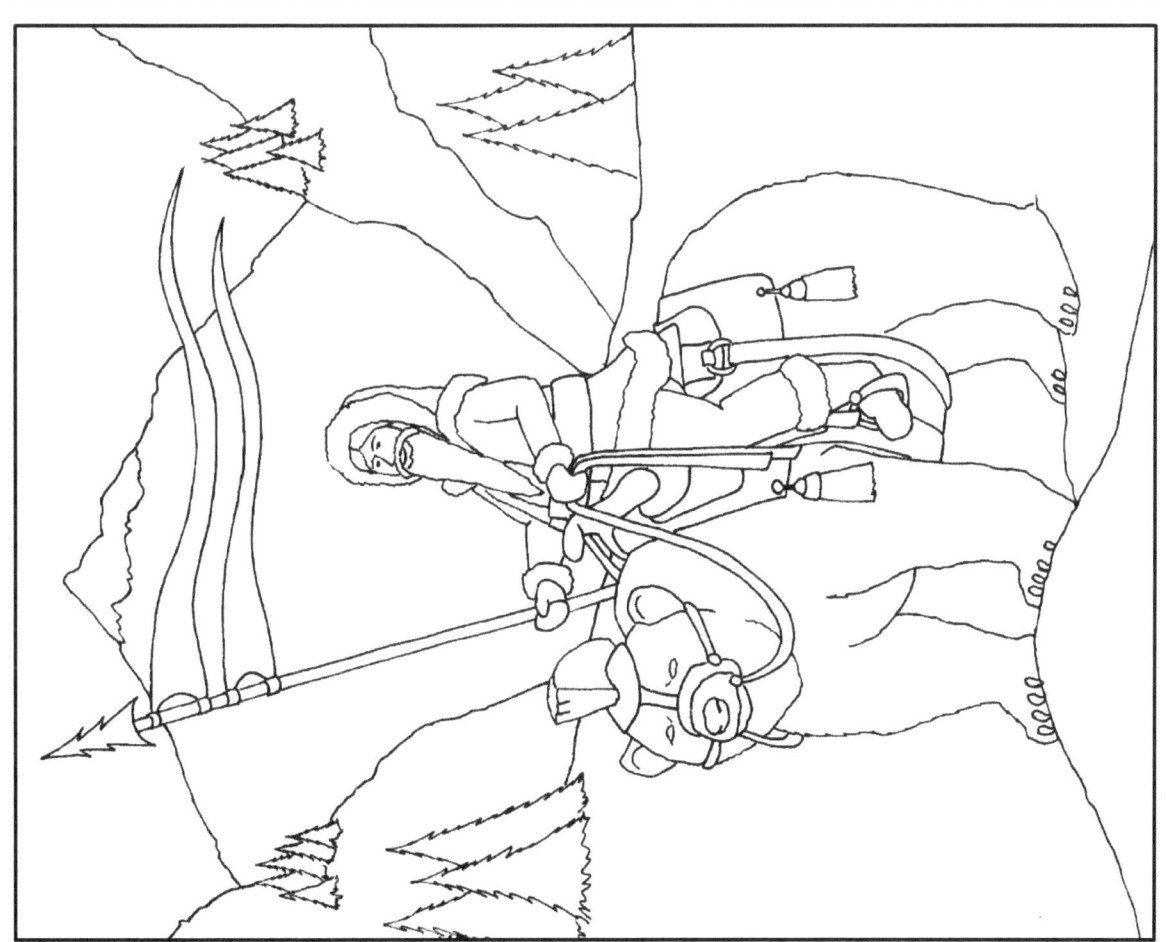

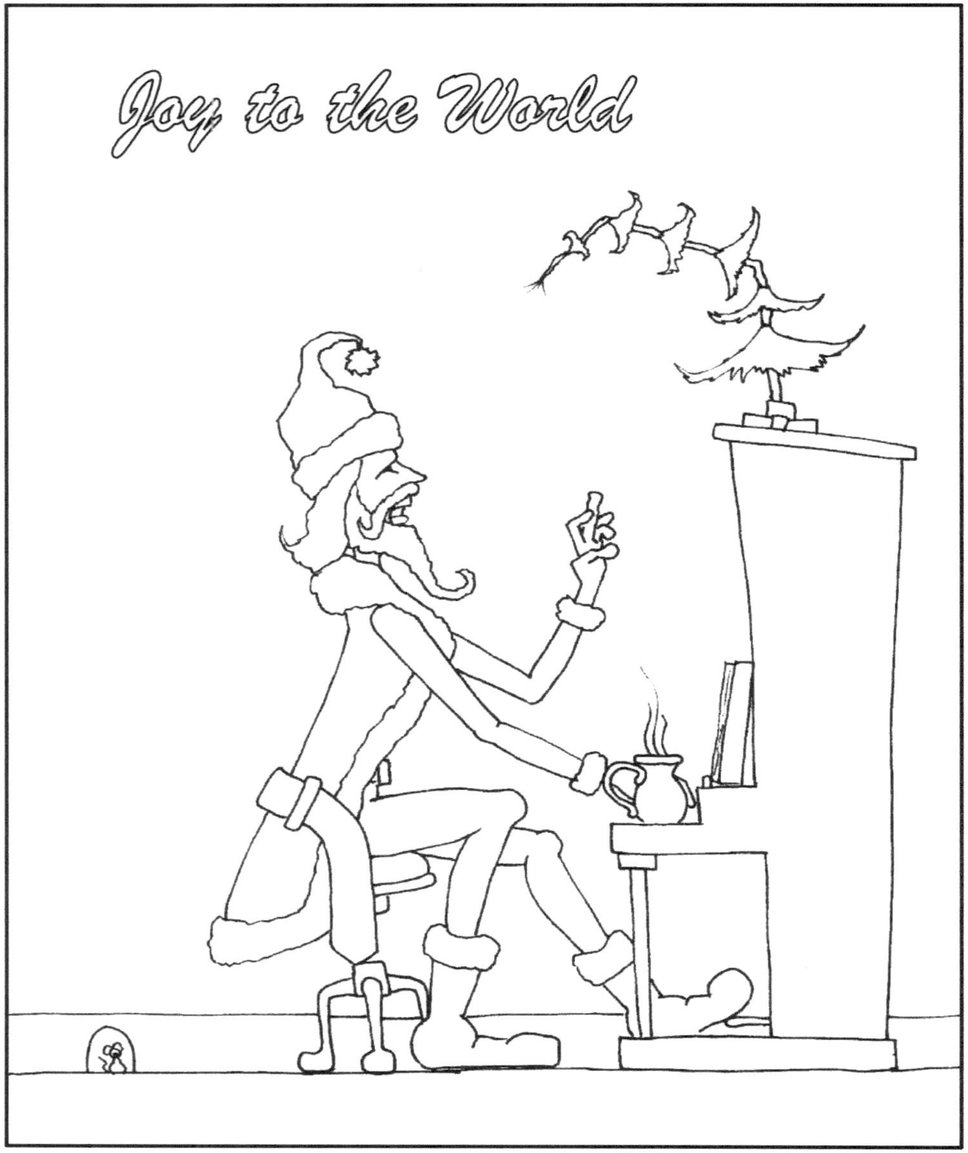

Joy to the World

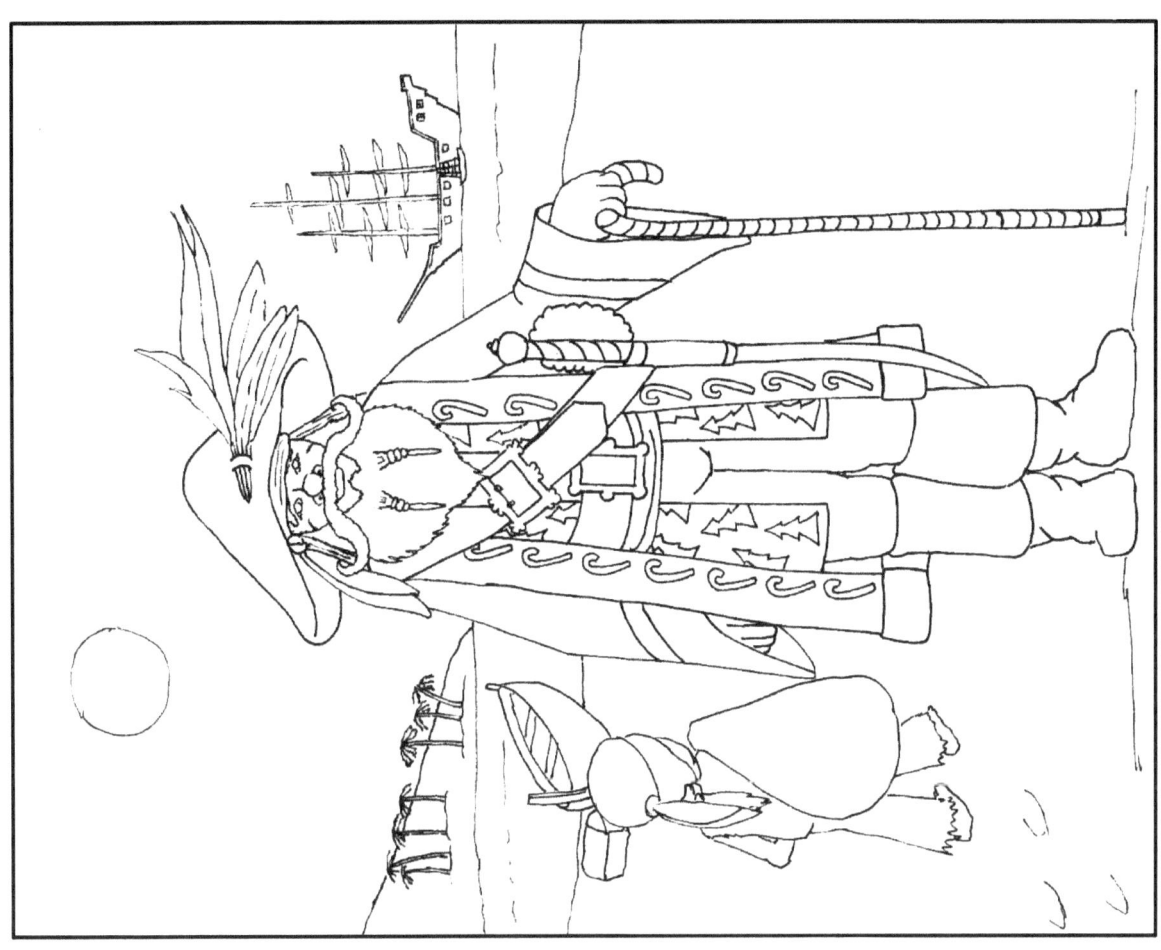
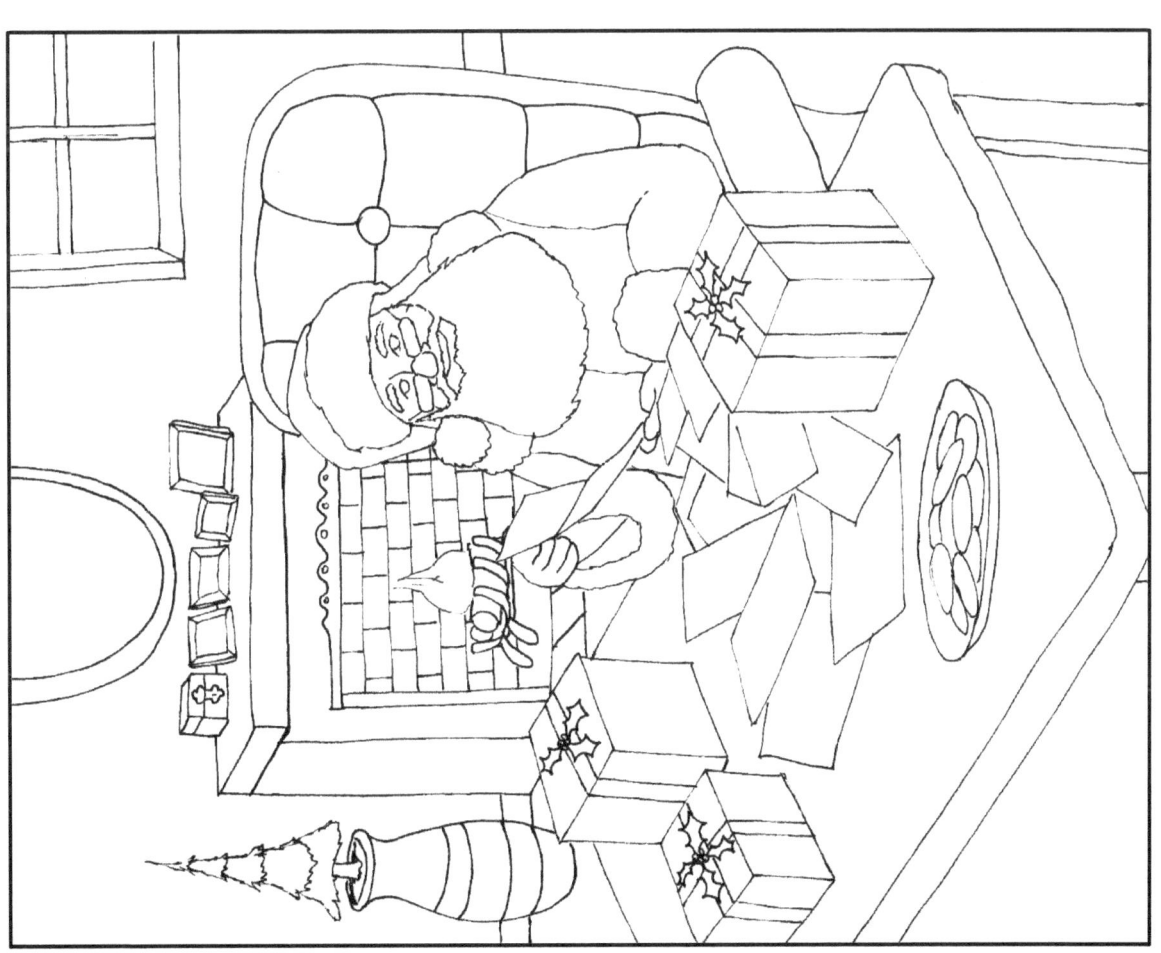

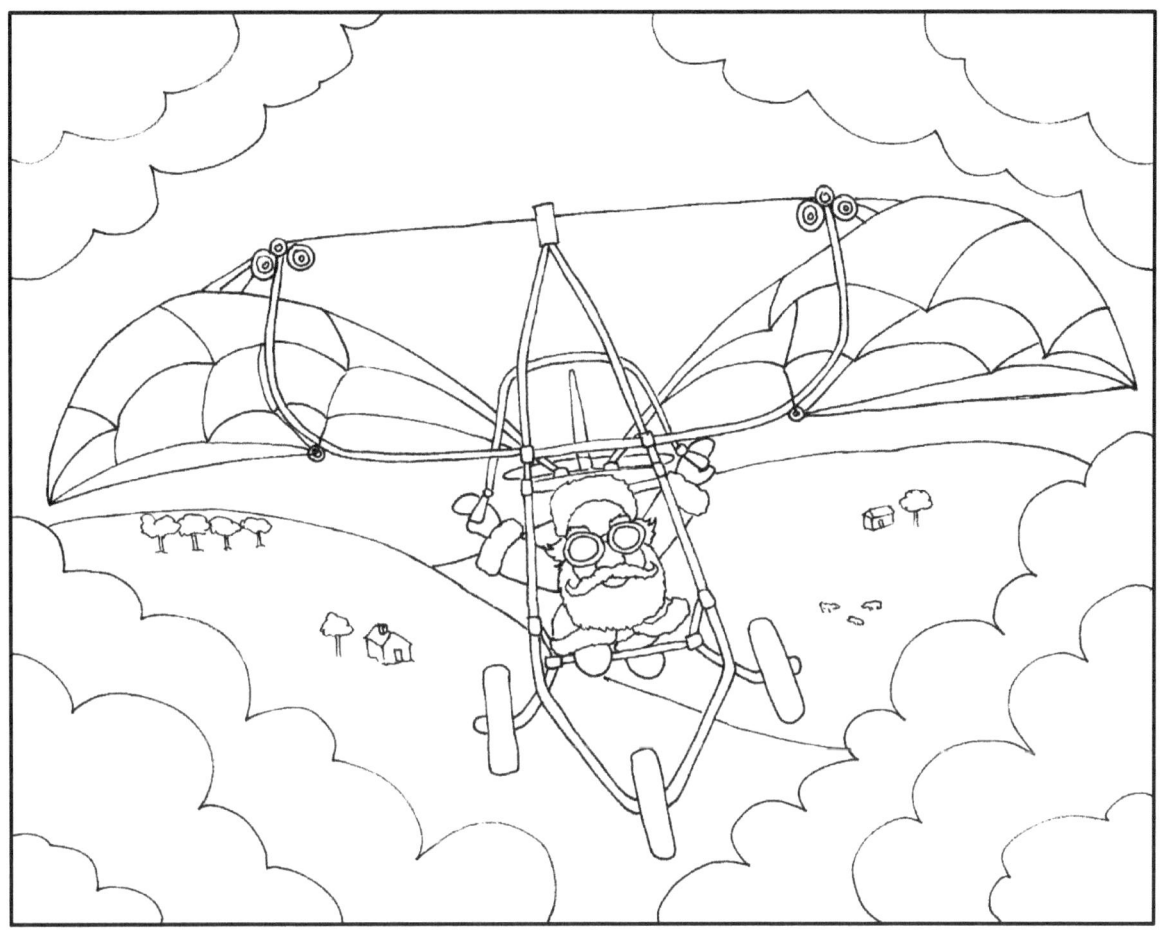
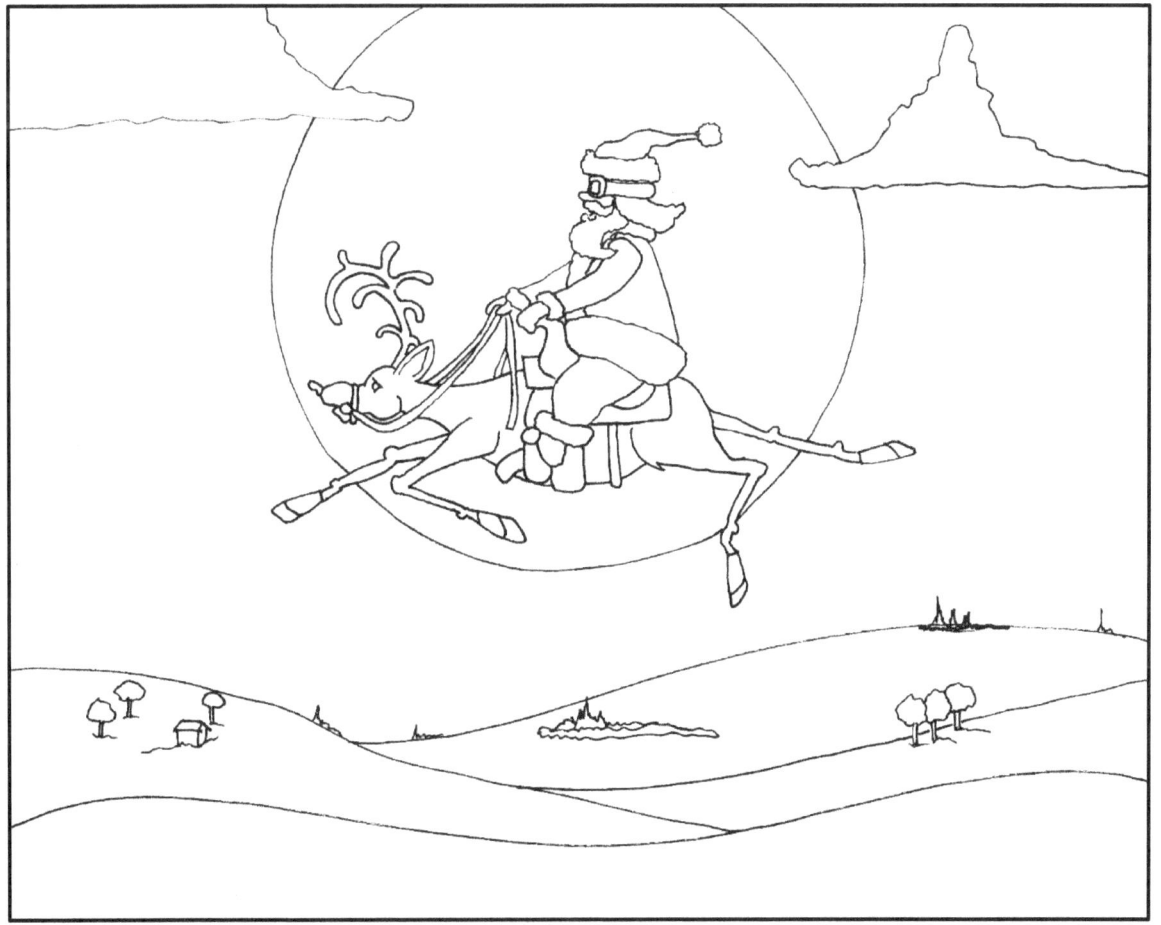

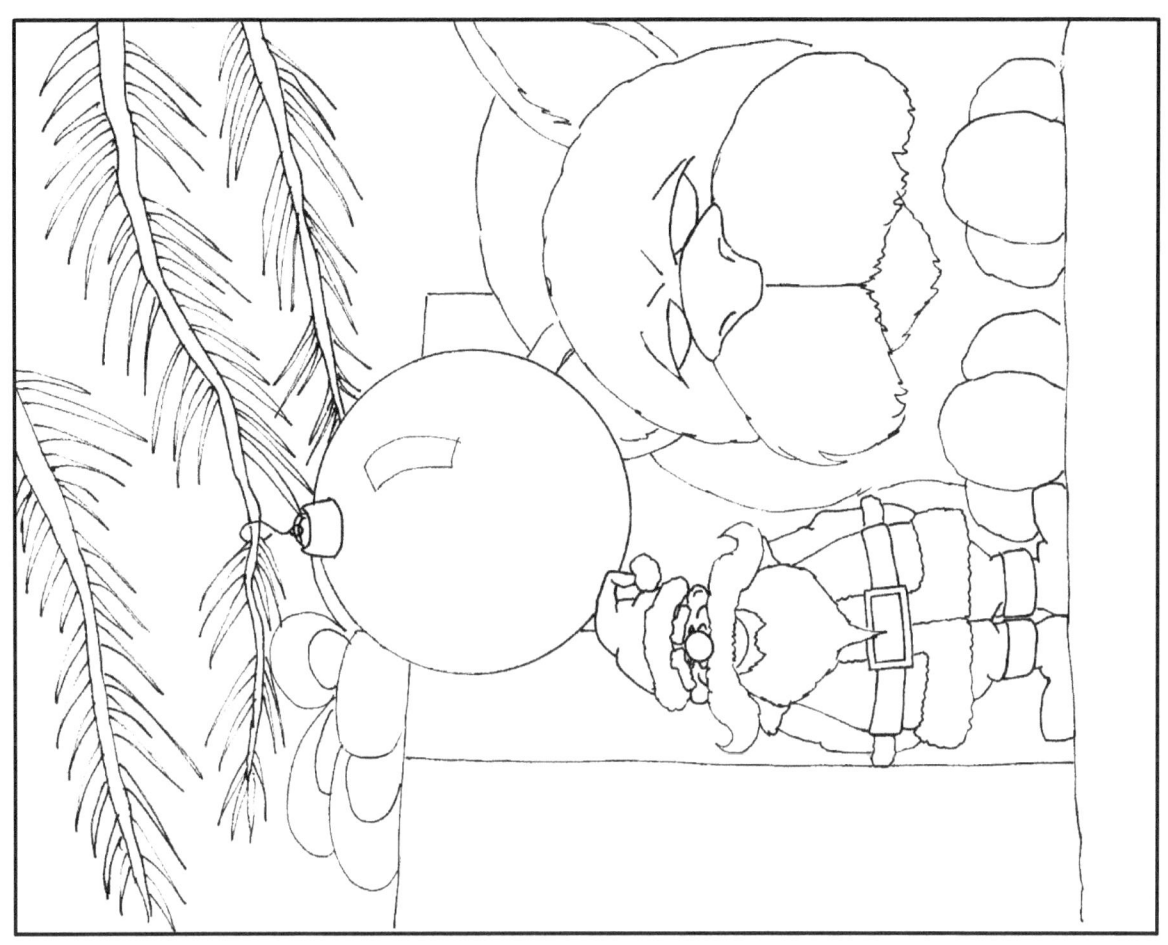
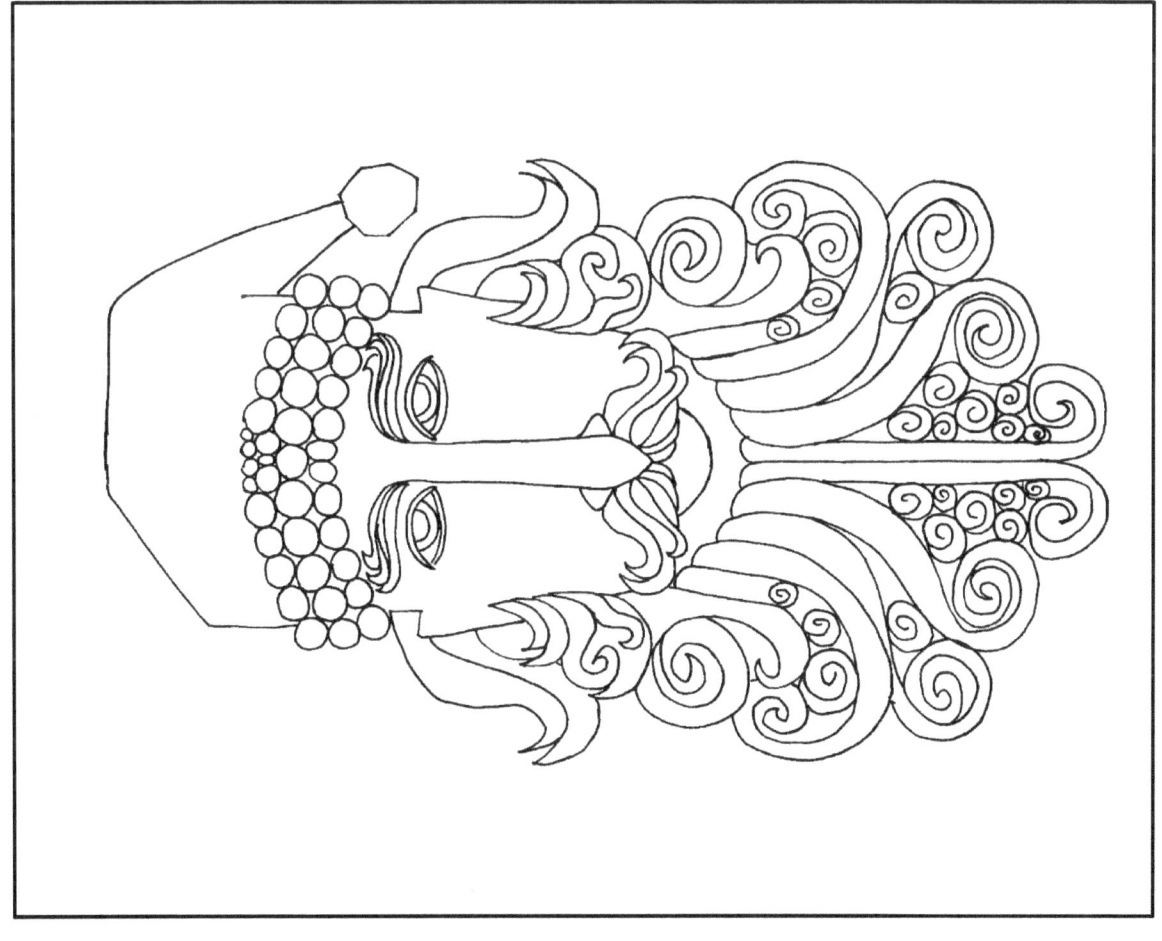

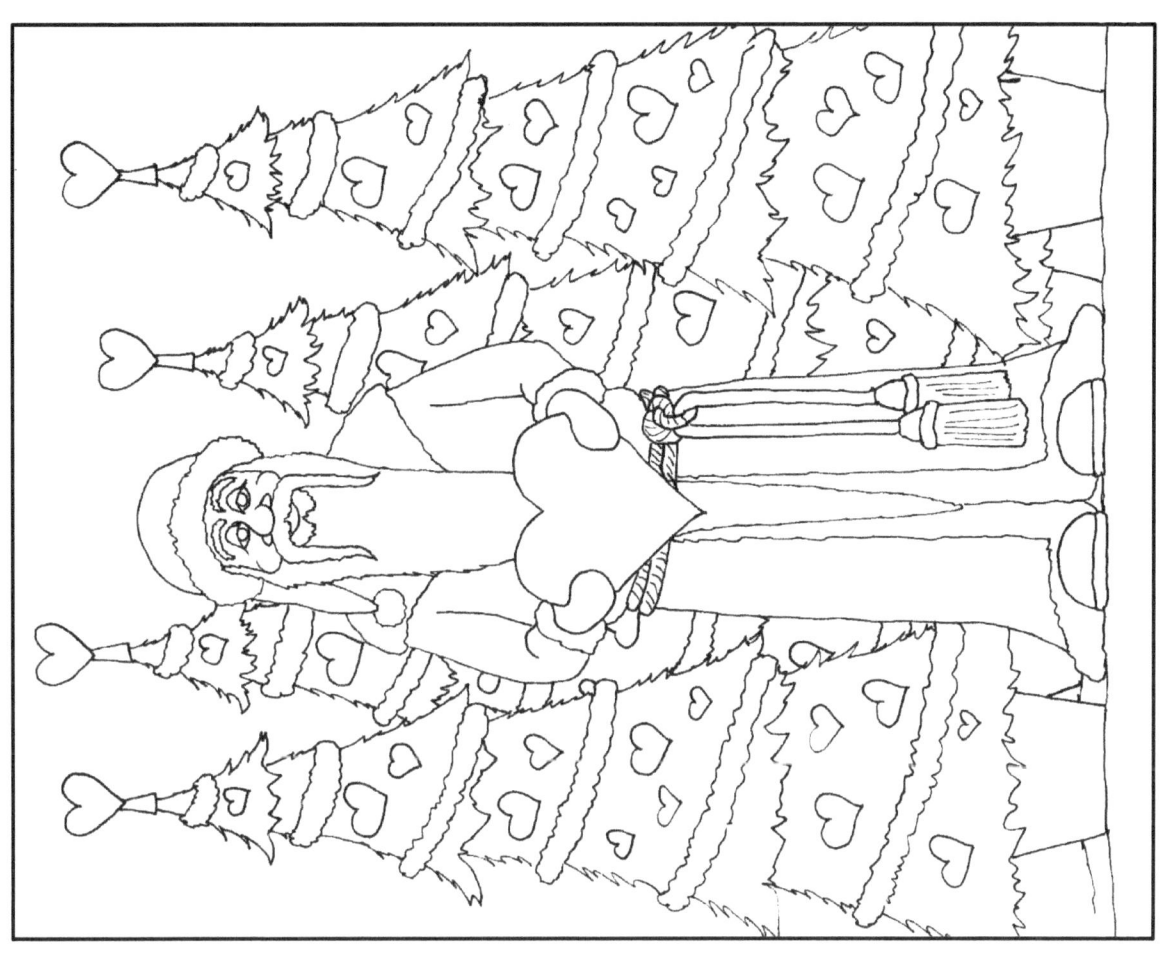
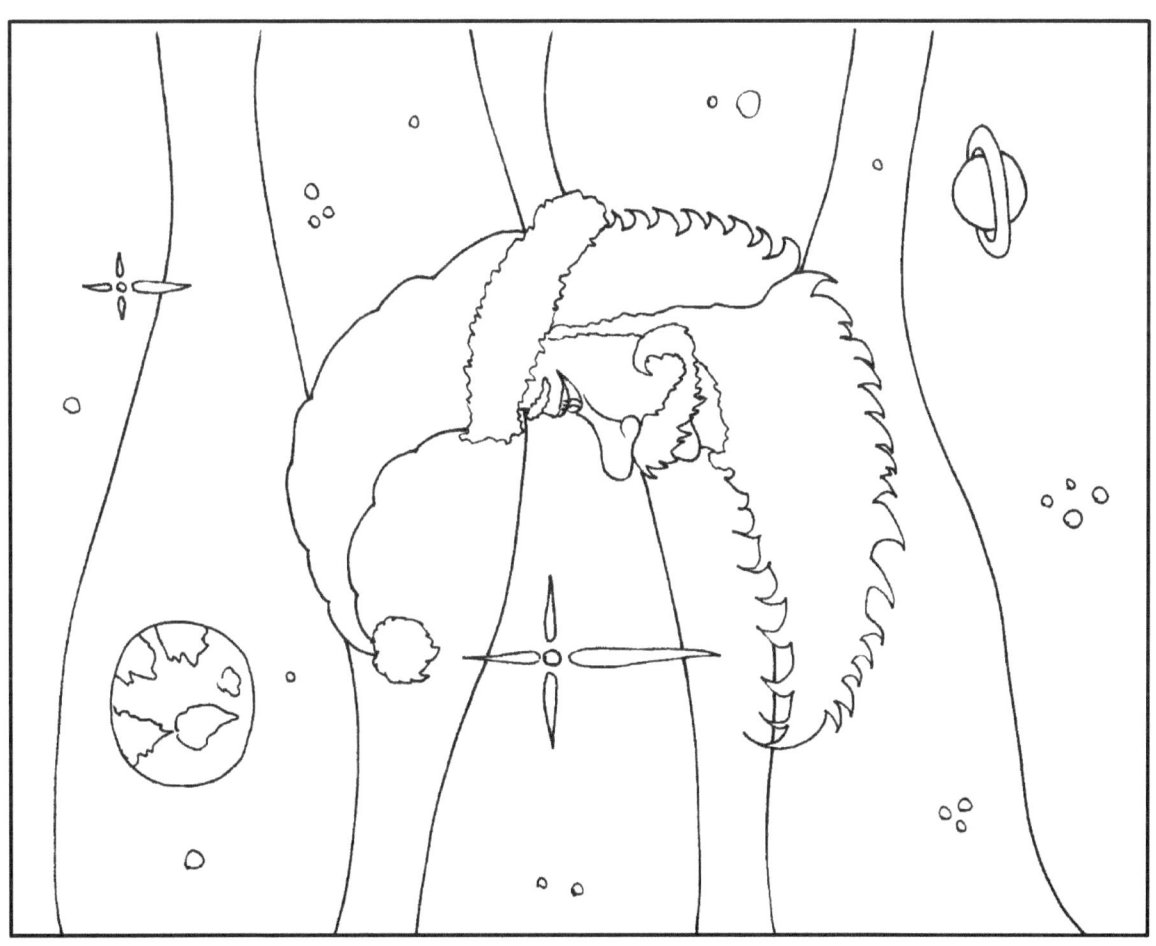

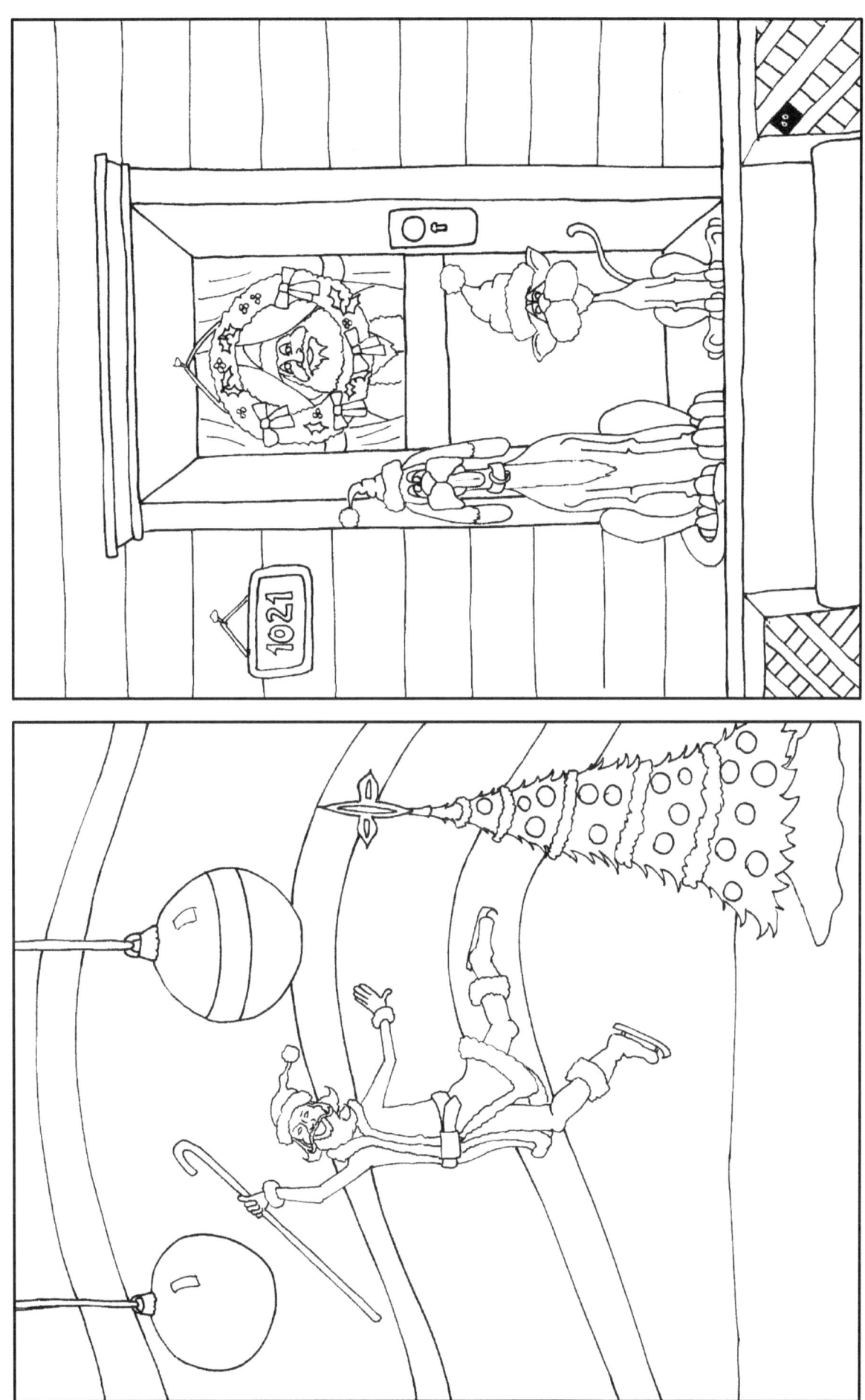

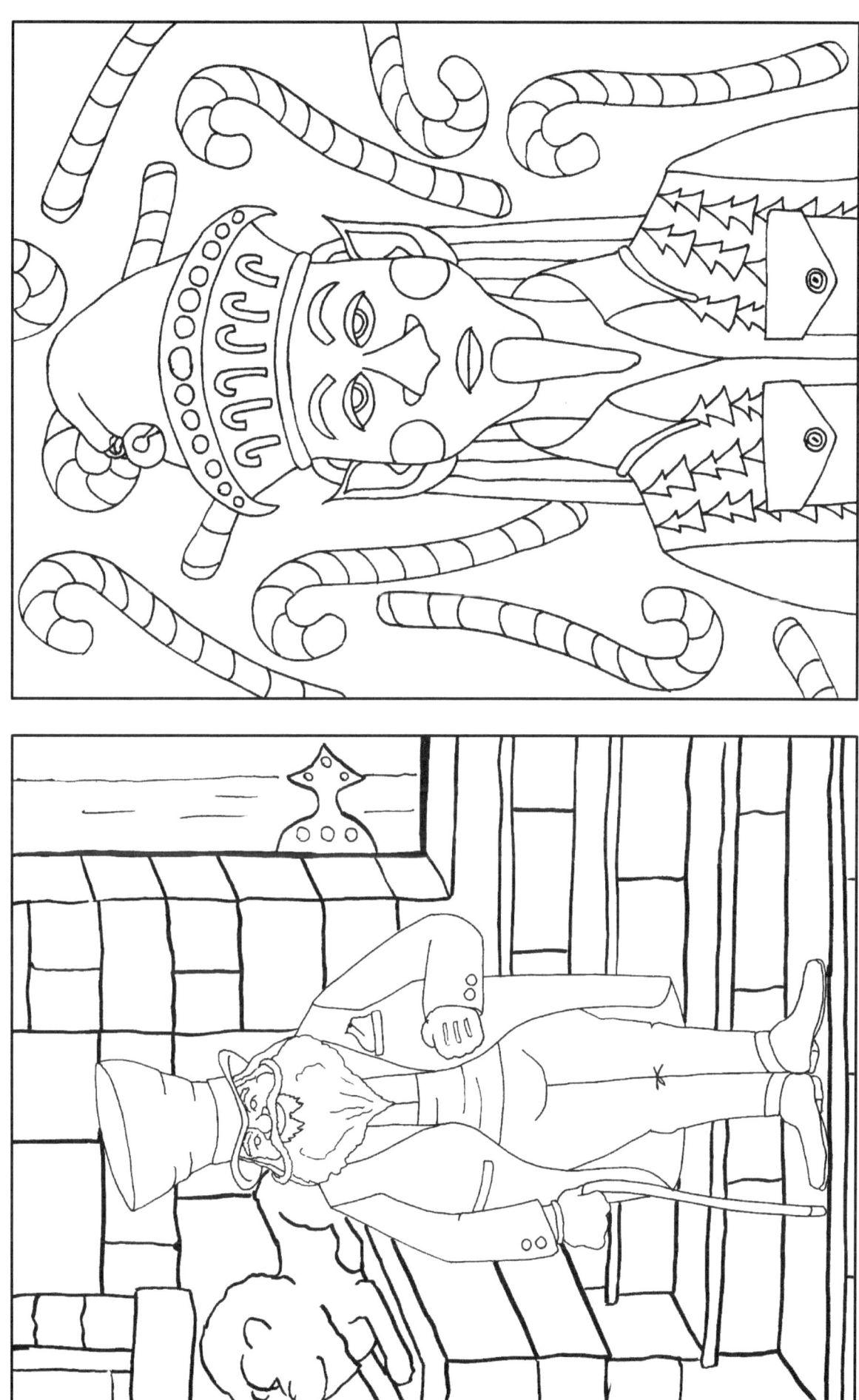

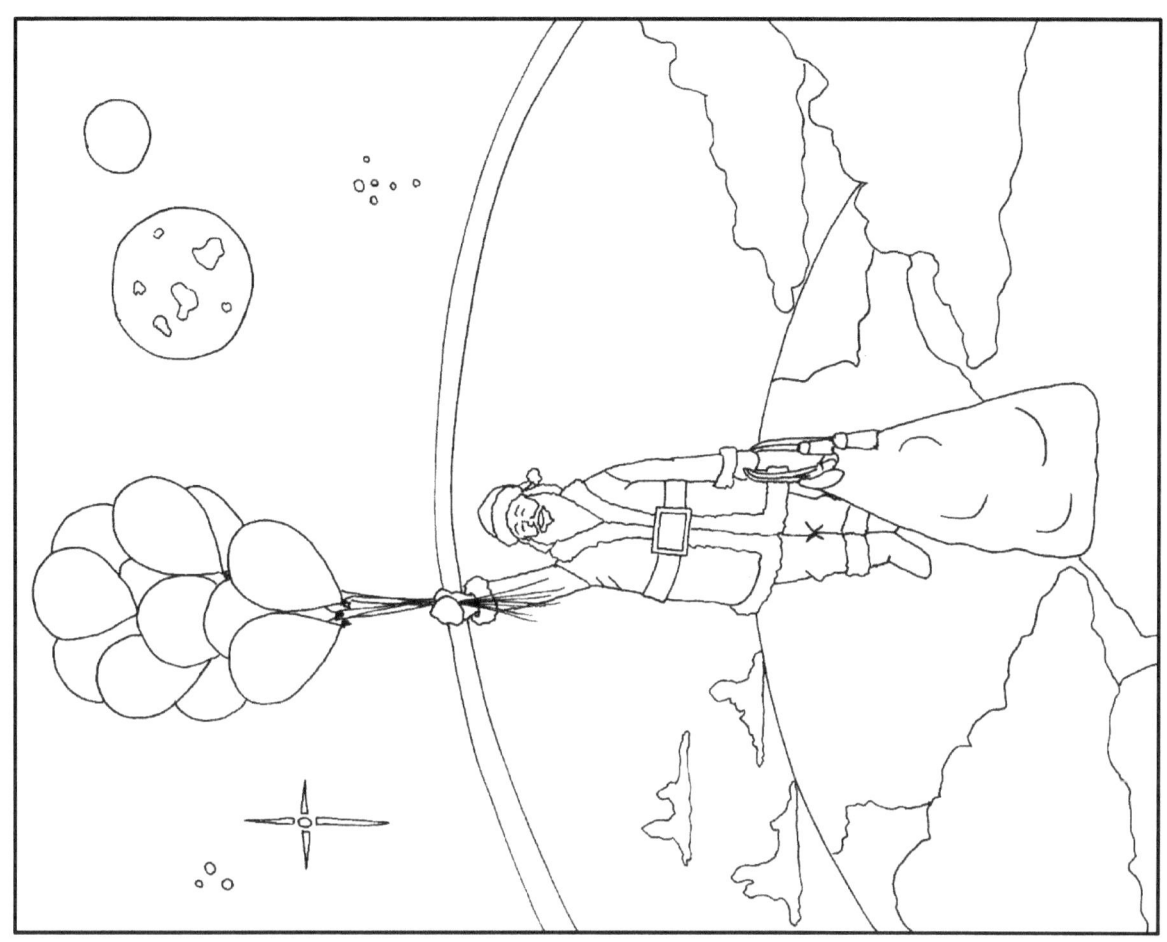
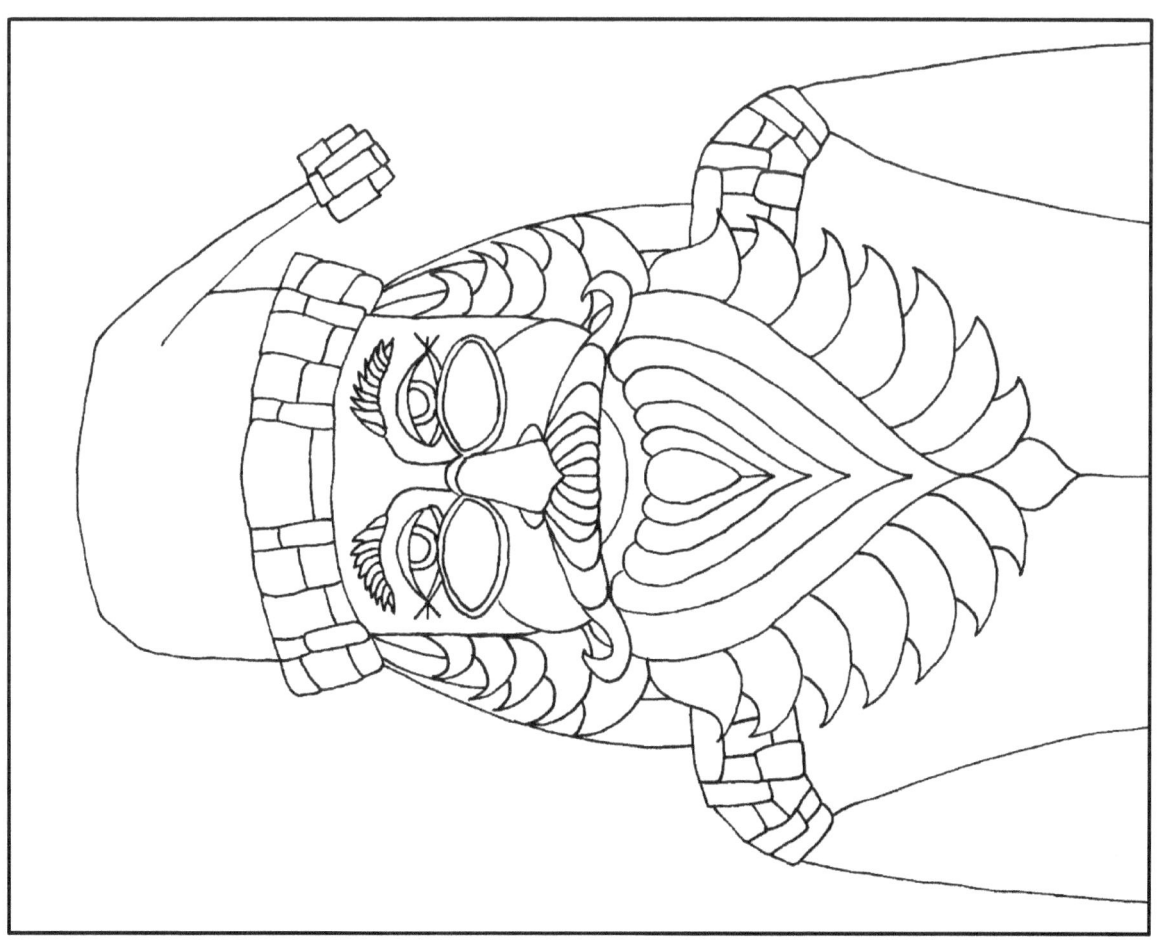

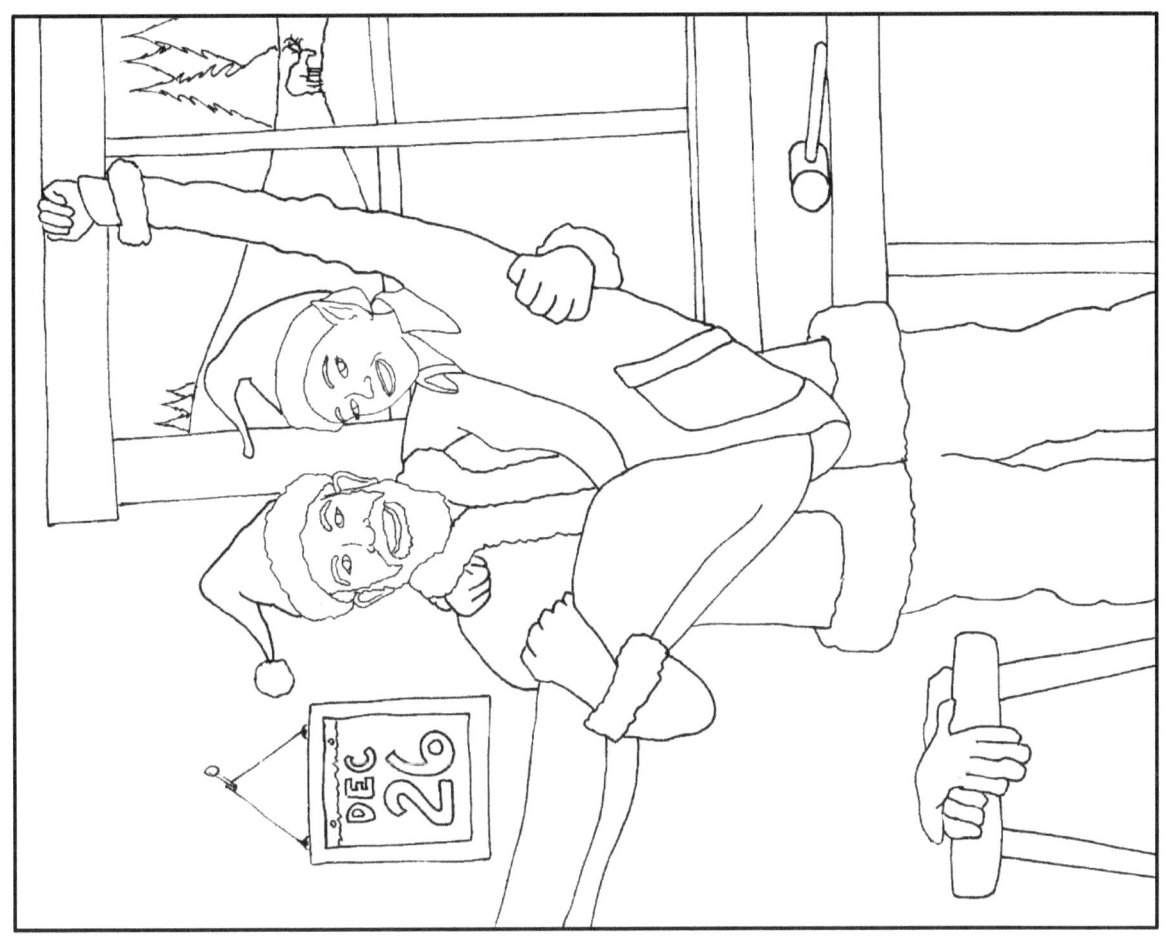
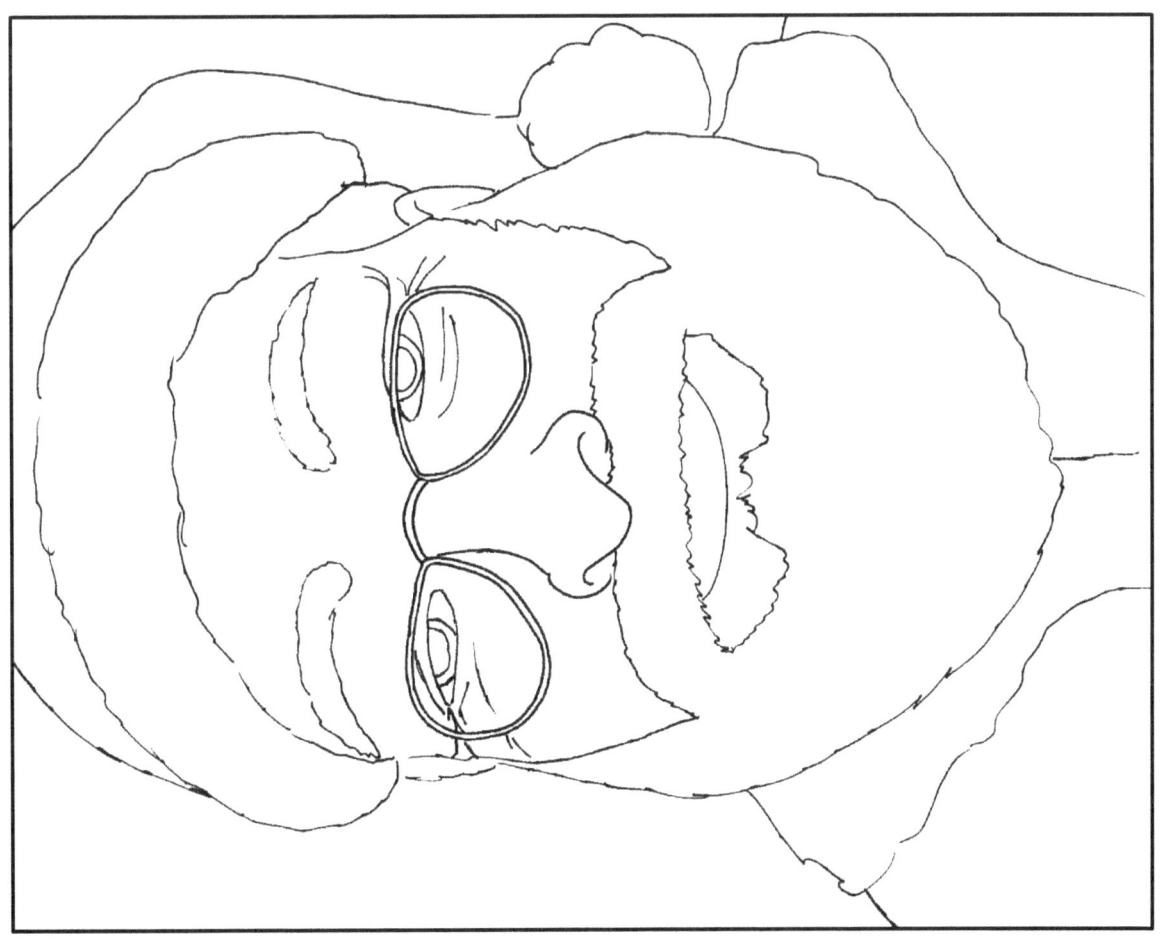

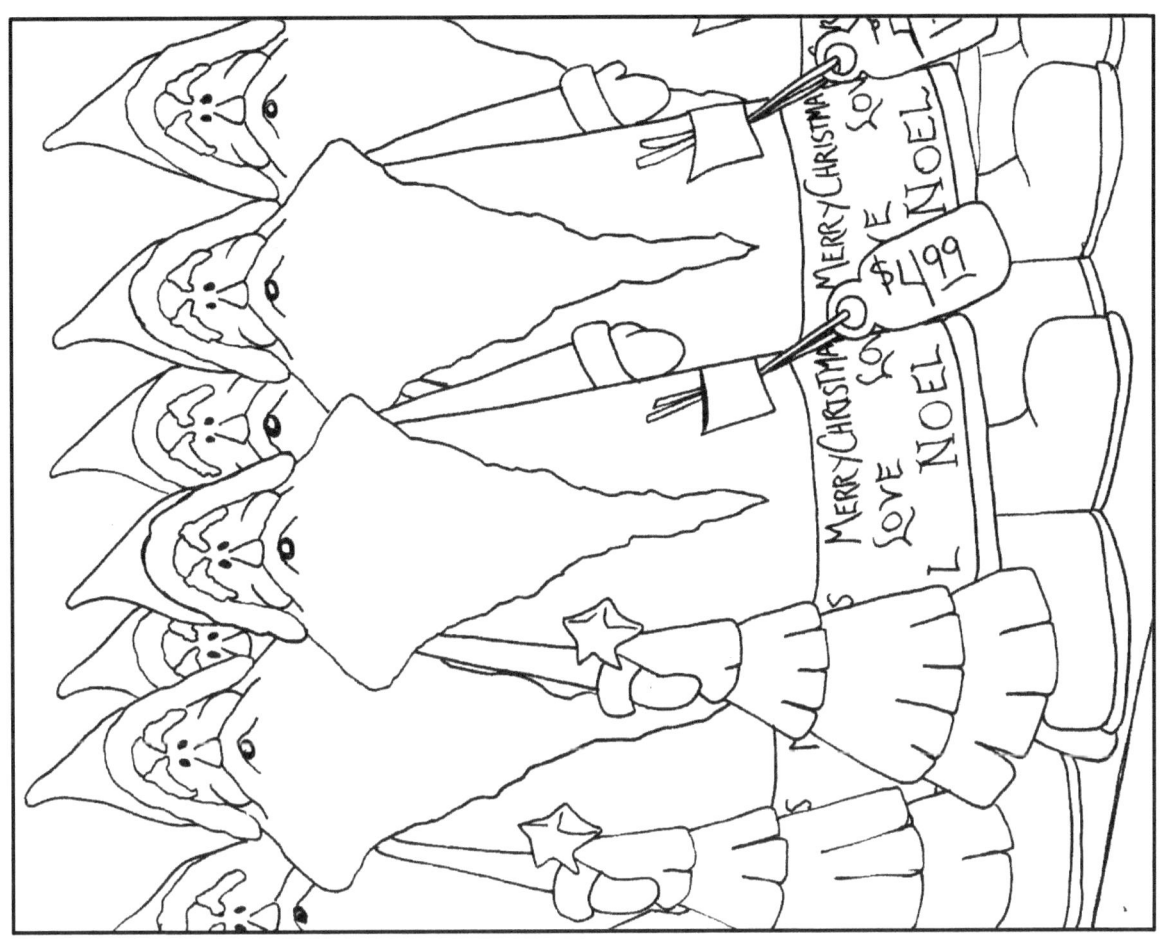
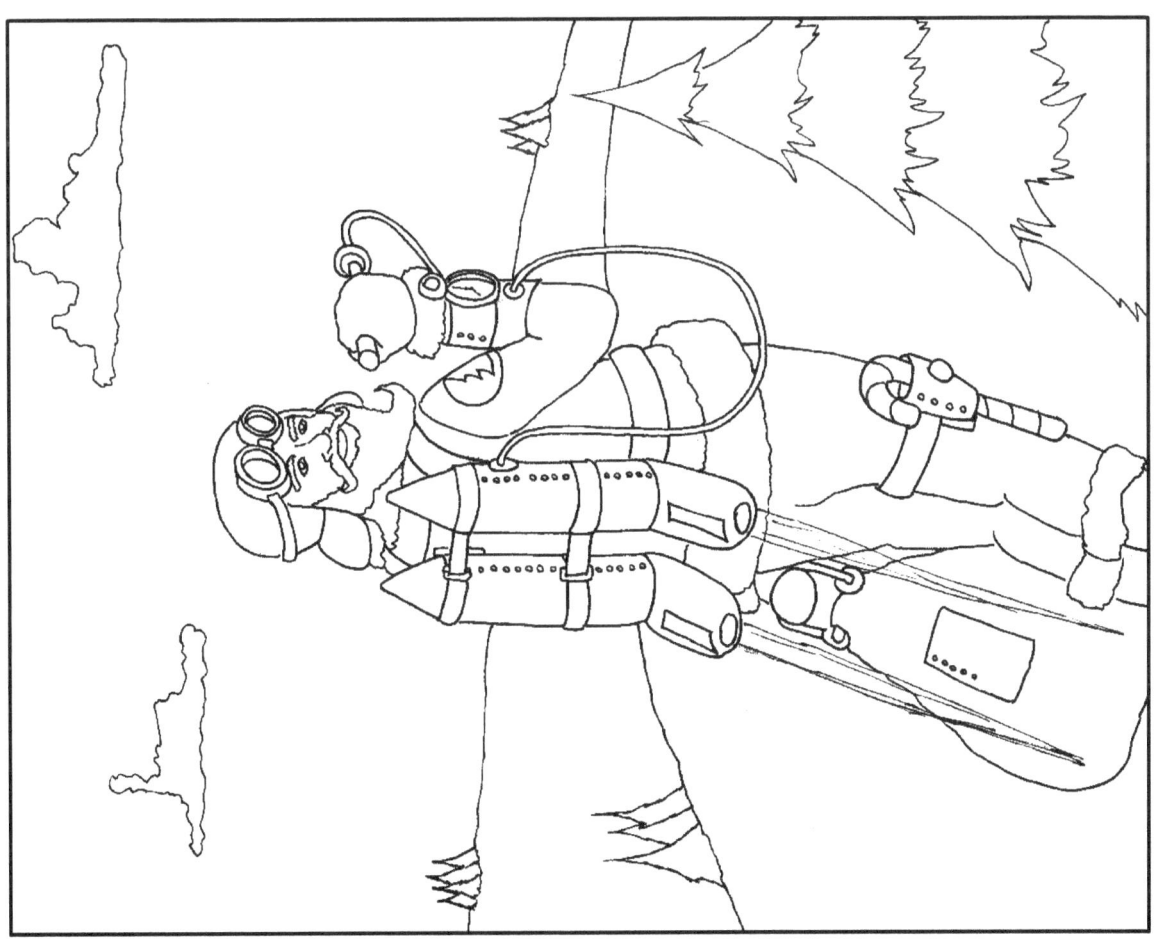

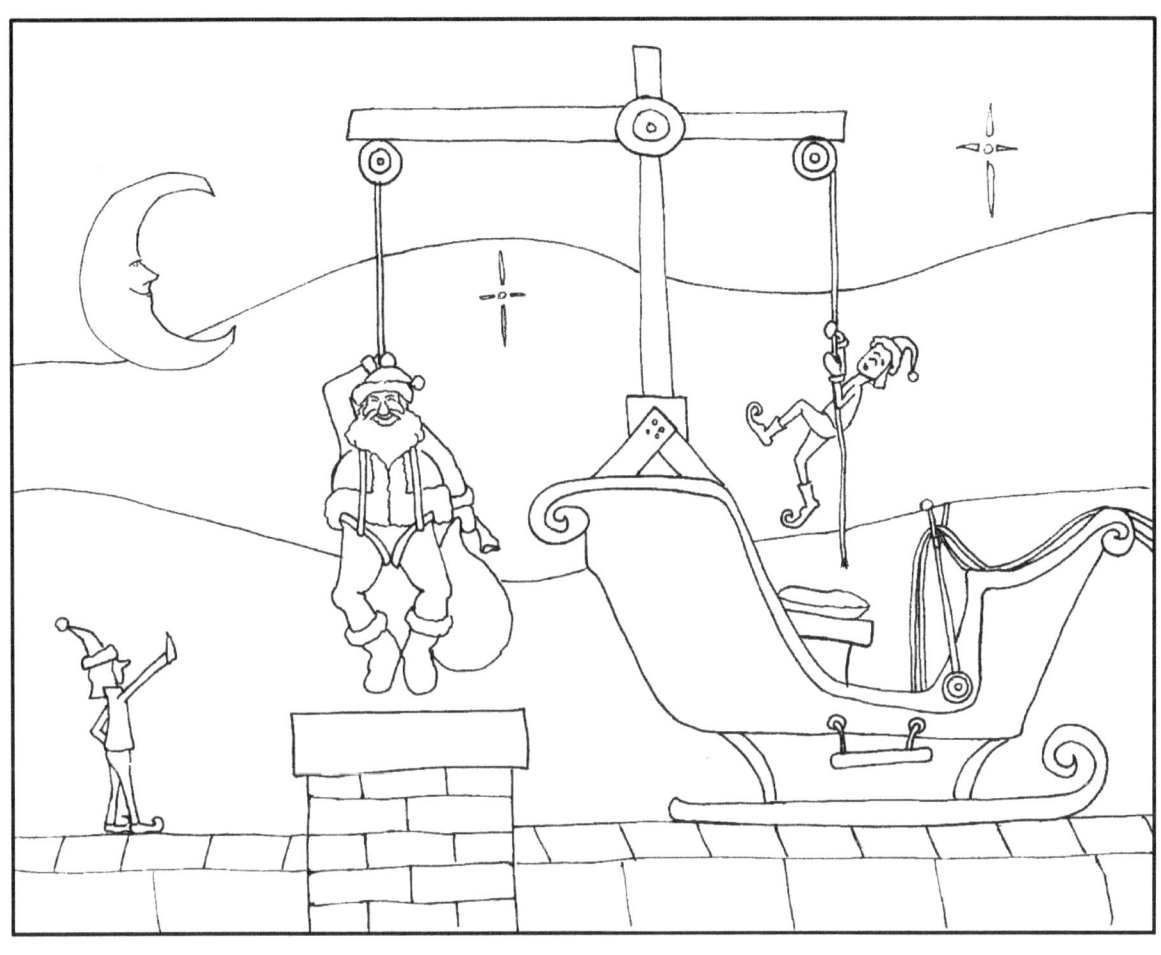
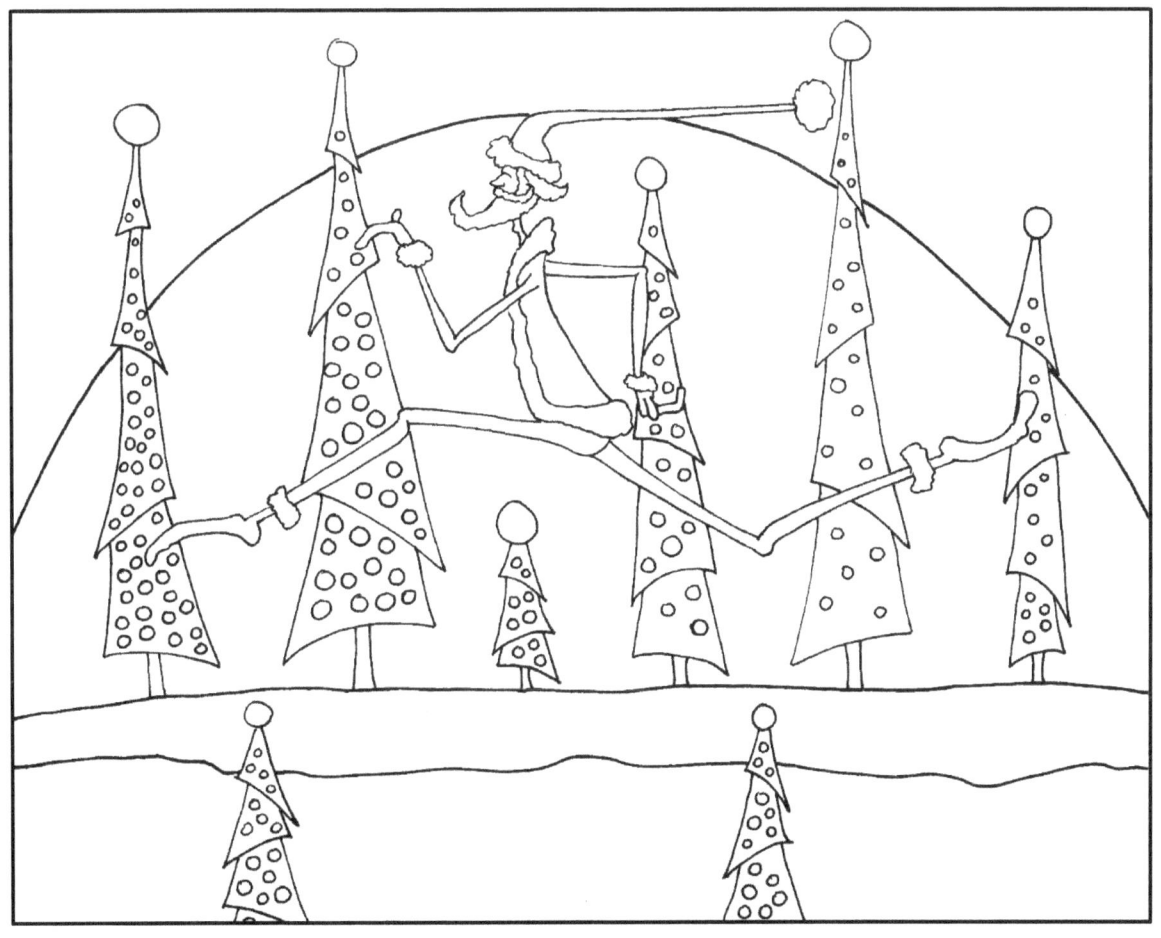

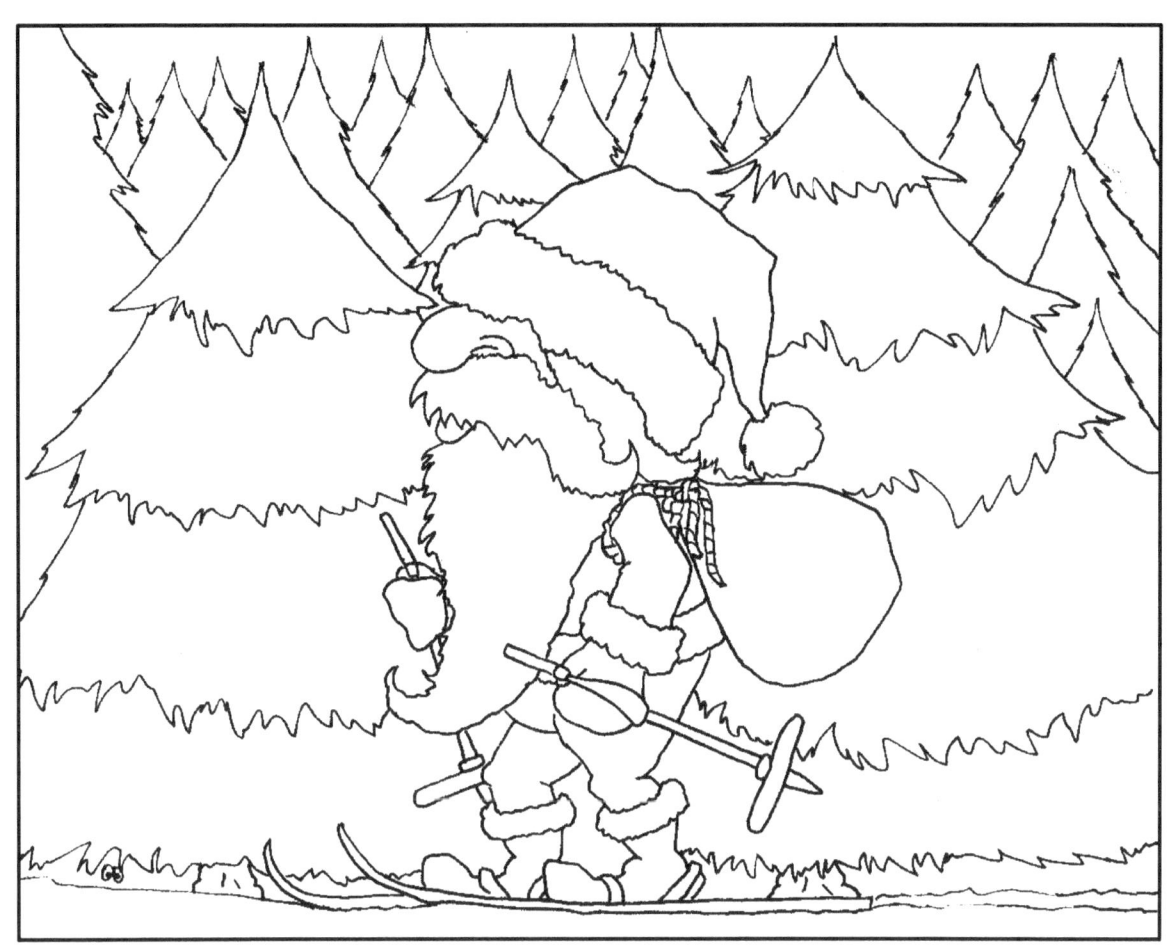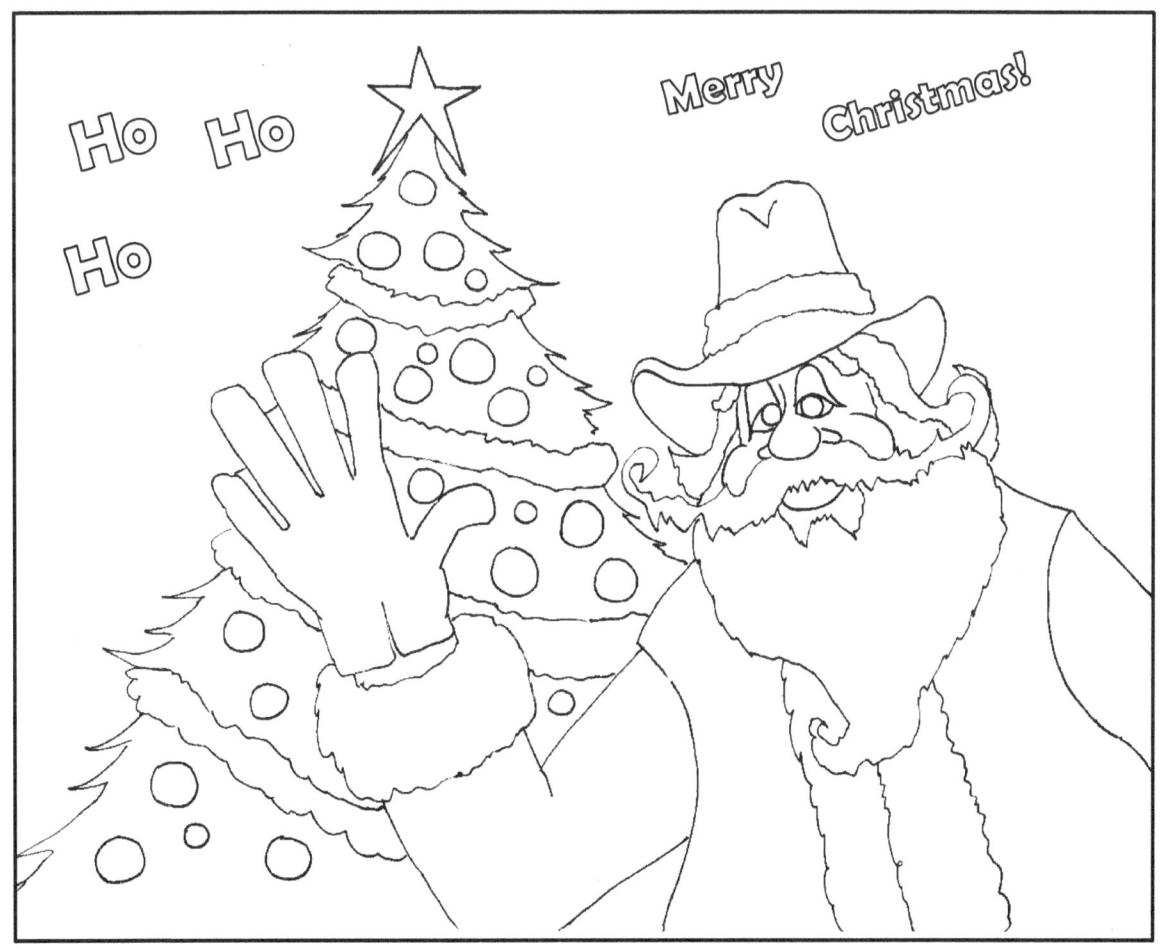

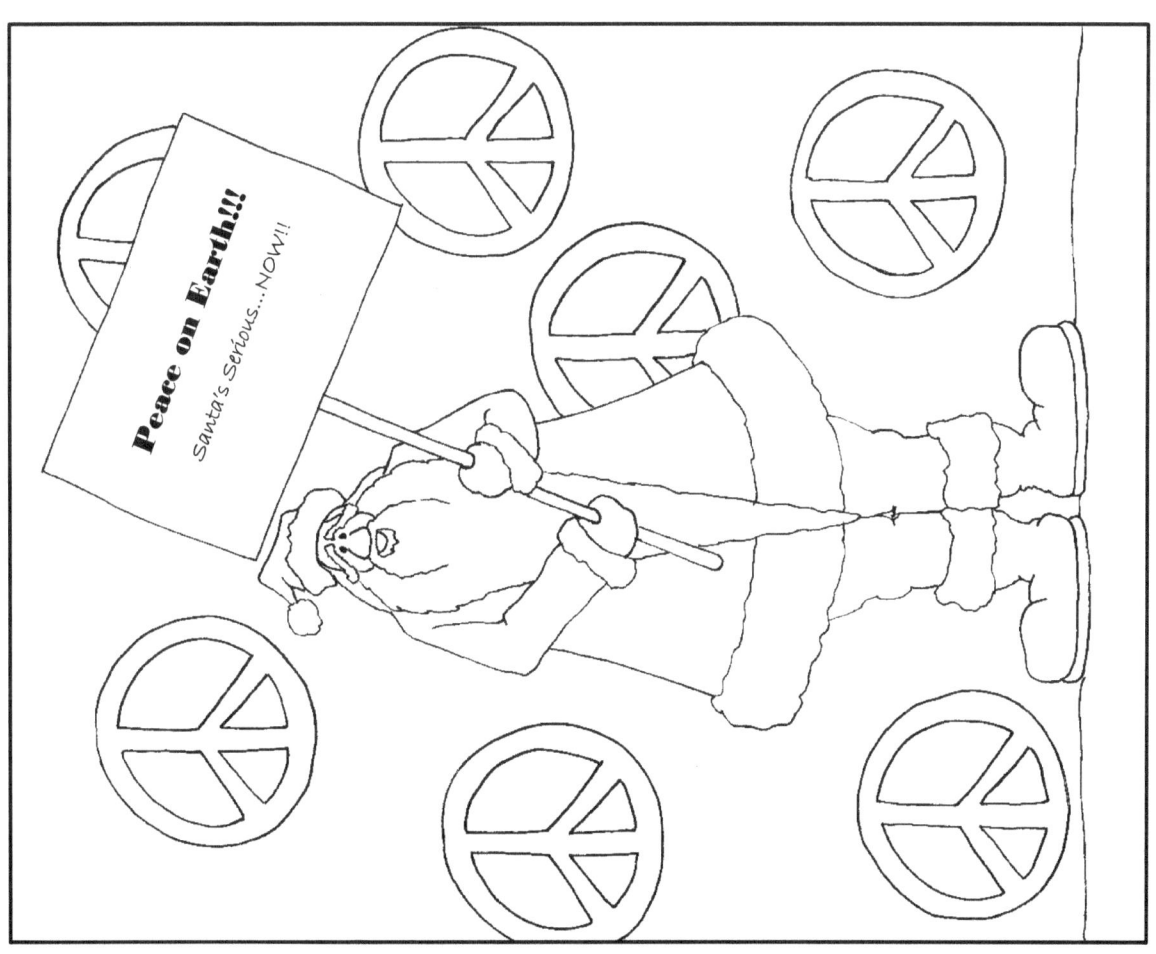

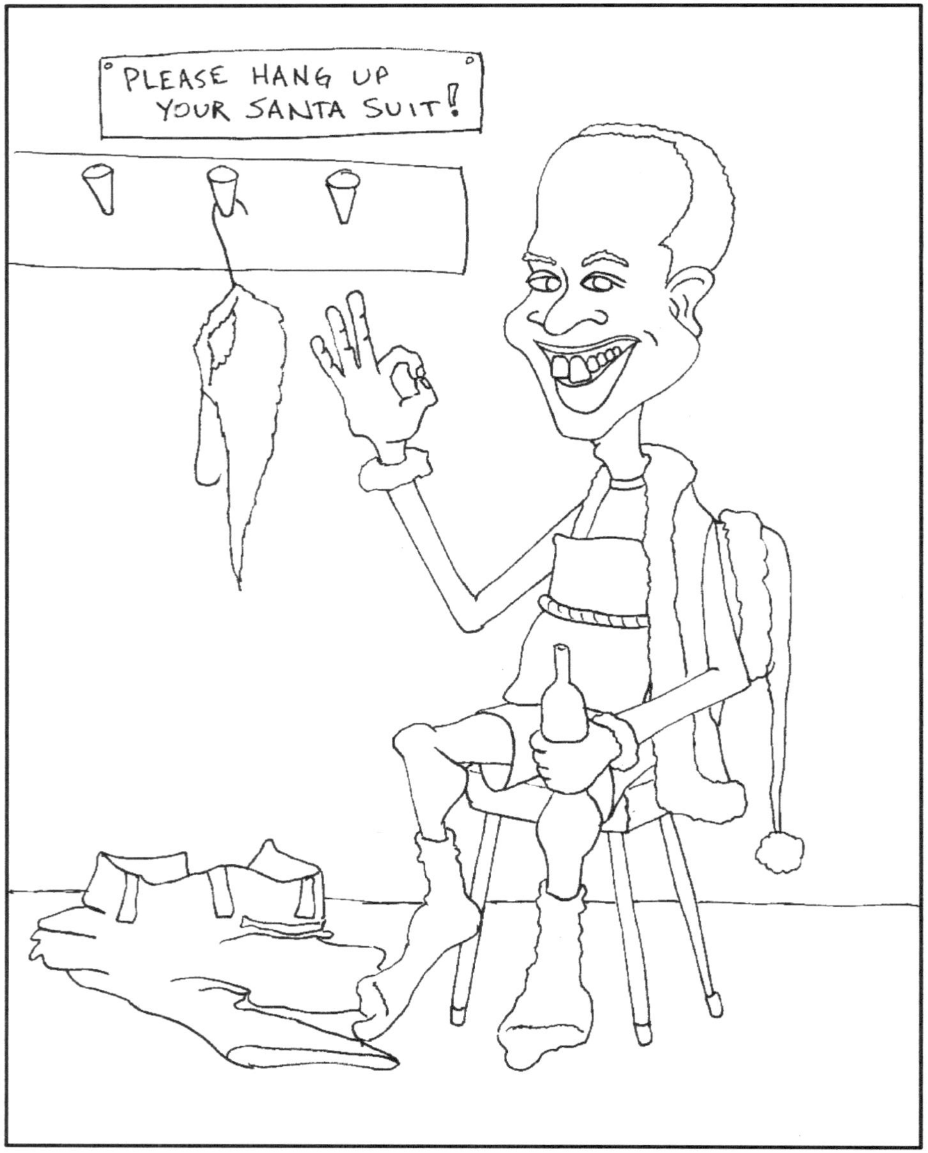

Bonus Pages from my other adult coloring book on Amazon

"Cats in Big Hats"

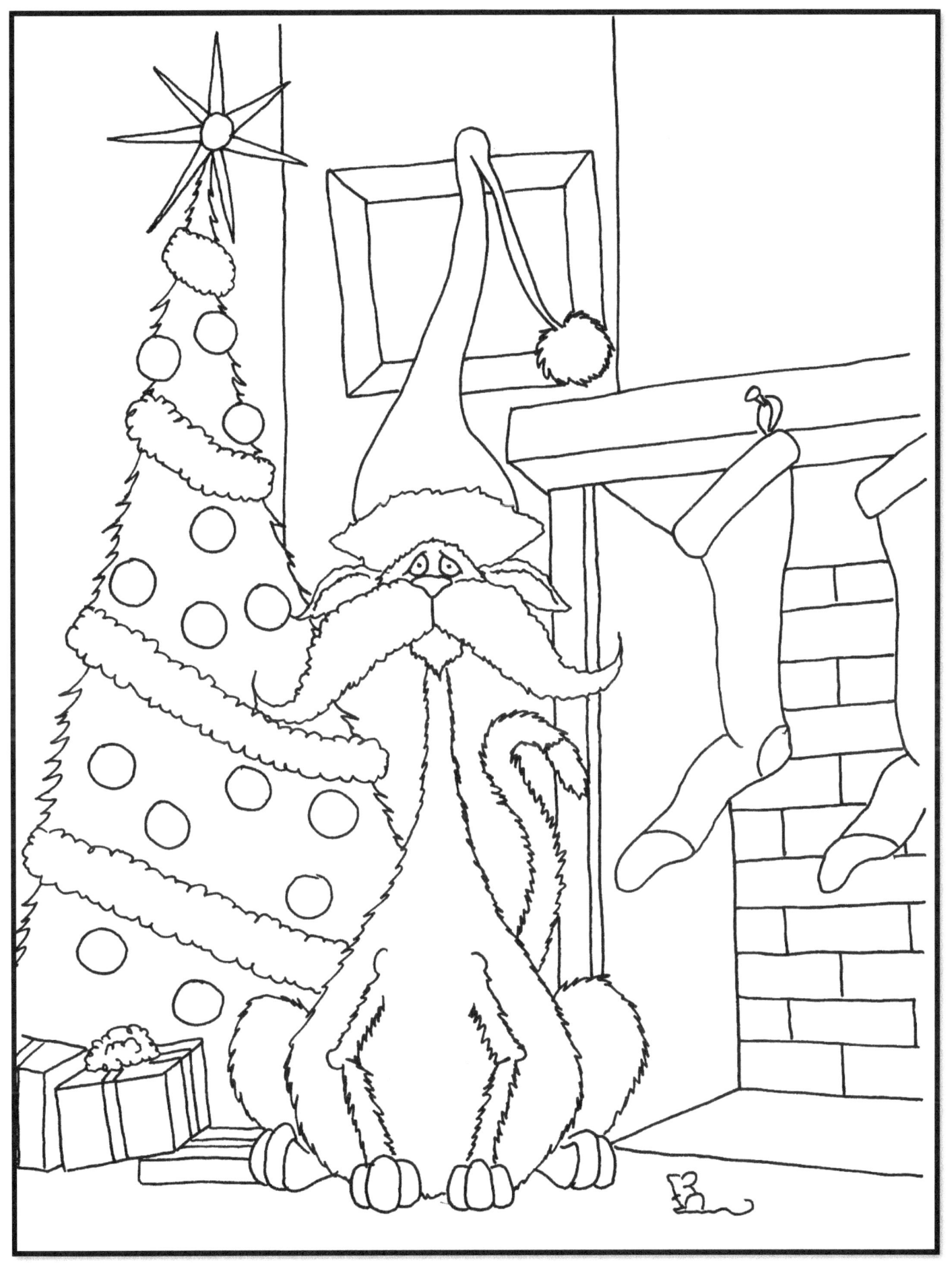

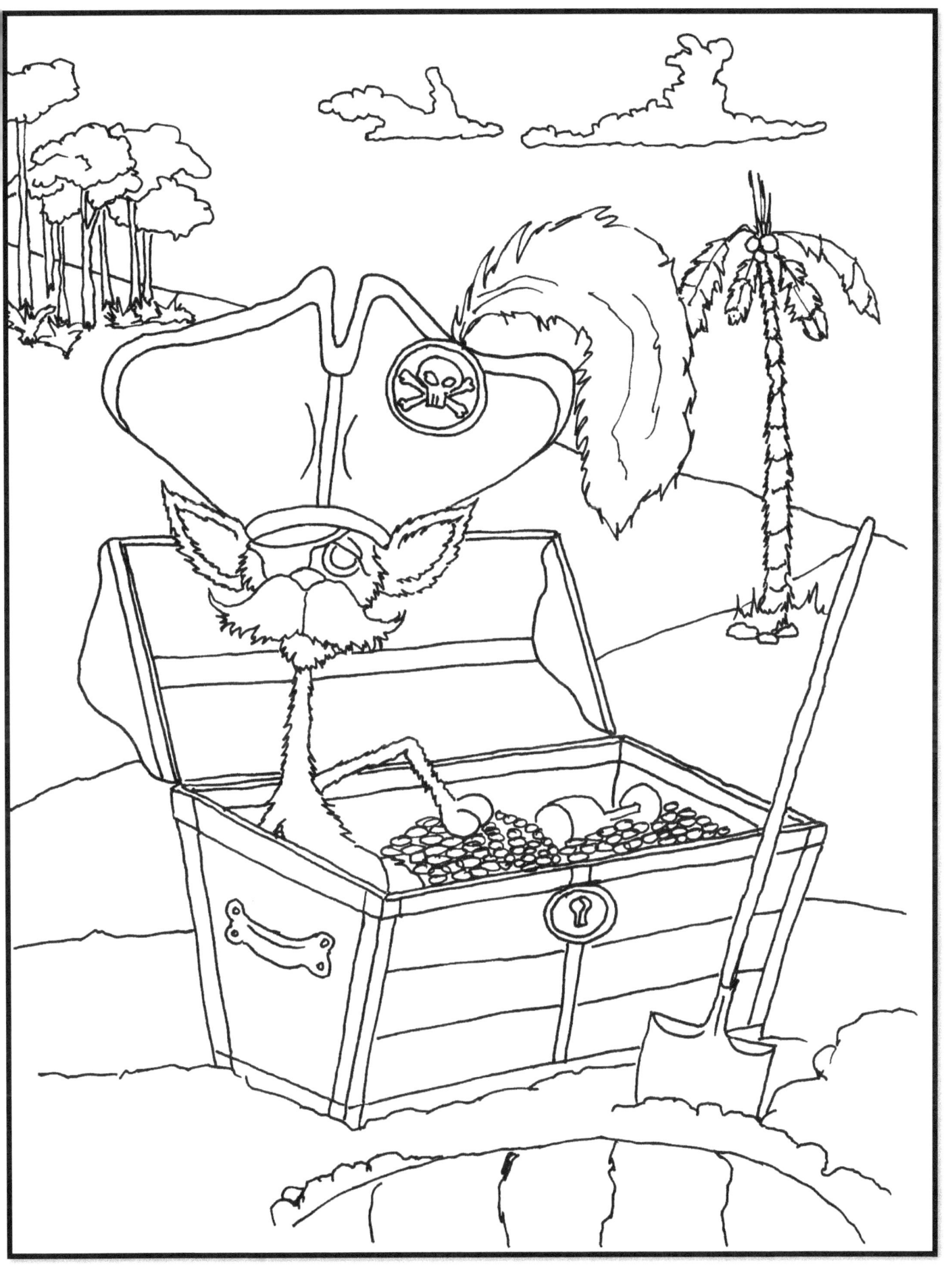

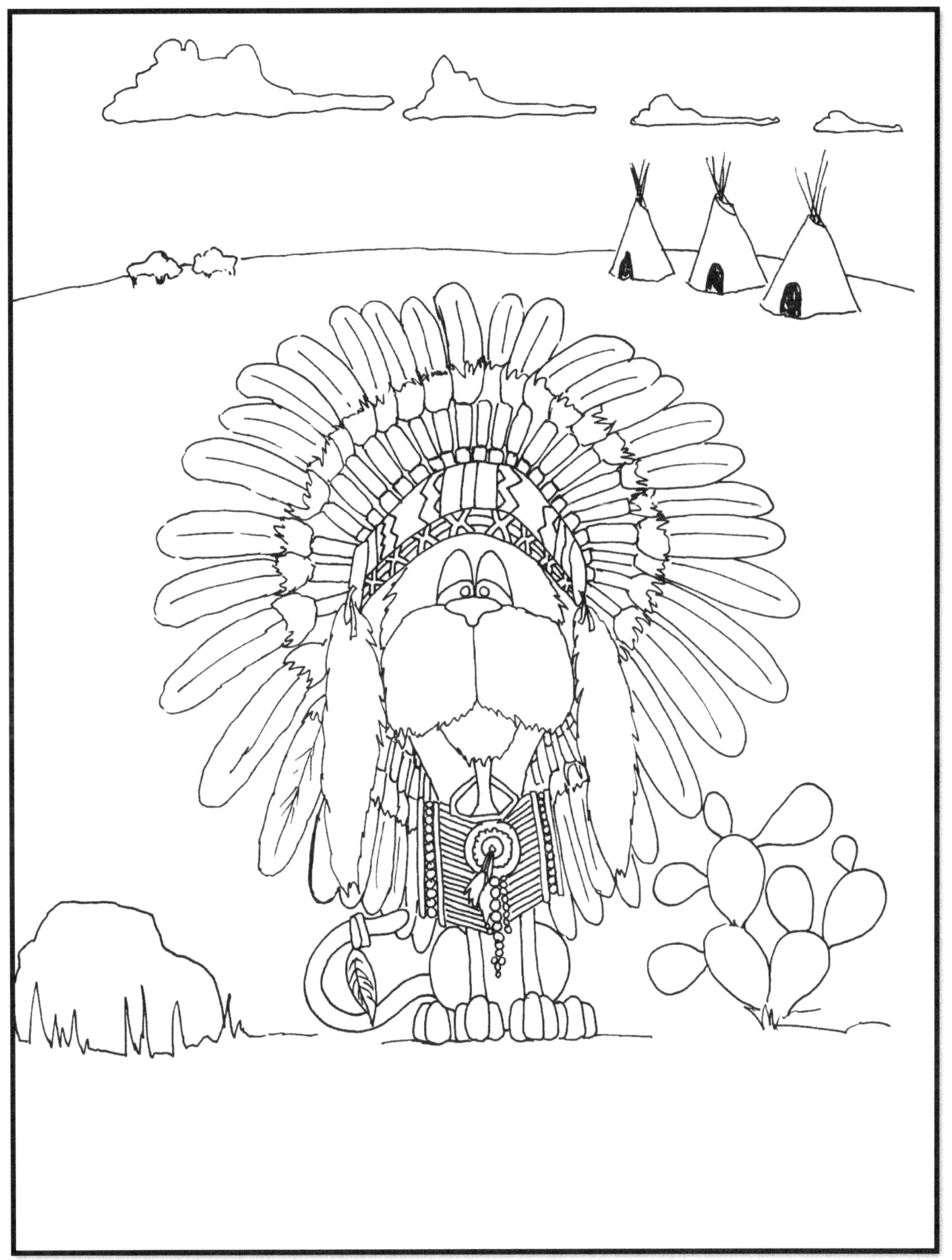

www.ingramcontent.com/pod-product-compliance
Lightning Source LLC
Chambersburg PA
CBHW062222220526
45471CB00009B/3309